R $_X$ for Worry

A Thankful Heart

Rx for Worry

A Thankful Heart

JAMES P. GILLS, M.D.

CREATION
HOUSE

R_X FOR WORRY by James P. Gills, M.D.
Published by Creation House
A Charisma Media Company
600 Rinehart Road
Lake Mary, FL 32746
www.creationhouse.com

Unless otherwise noted, Scripture quotations are from The Holy Bible, New International Version. Copyright © 1973, 1978, 1984 by the International Bible Society. Used by permission of Zondervan Publishing House. All rights reserved.

Scripture quotations marked NAS are from the New American Standard Bible—Updated Edition. Copyright © 1960, 1962, 1963, 1968, 1971, 1972, 1973, 1975, 1977, 1995 by The Lockman Foundation. Used by permission.

Scripture quotations marked NKJV are from the New King James Version of the Bible. Copyright © 1979, 1980, 1982 by Thomas Nelson, Inc., publishers. Used by permission.

Excerpts from the book, *Future Grace*, by John Piper; Multnomah Publishers, Inc., copyright © 1995. Used by permission.

Original edition of *Rx for Worry* was published by Creation House, Lake Mary, FL, 2002, ISBN 0-88419-932-0.

Cover design by Terry Clifton

Library of Congress Control Number: 2006936880
International Standard Book Number: 978-1-59979-090-9
E-Book ISBN: 978-1-59979-926-1

15 16 17 18 19 — 9 8 7 6 5 4 3 2

Printed in the United States of America

I dedicate this book to all those who struggle in the war against worry. May each of us find peace by resting and rejoicing in the promises of God.

ACKNOWLEDGMENTS

THIS BOOK COULD not have been written without my good friend and colleague, Gary Carter. Gary's insight, wisdom, and sense of God's joy have guided us through countless discussions about the thorny issues of worry and faith. He has been an invaluable partner in prayer and praise throughout the writing of this book.

I am also deeply grateful to the staff members at St. Luke's Cataract and Laser Institute for their support and timely words of encouragement. Special thanks go to Lois Babcock for her commitment to this project. And I owe much to the patients at St. Luke's, who have shown me valuable lessons in trust.

My wife, Heather, continues to be a source of strength and support. Her love, rooted in the love of God, is an inspiration to me.

CONTENTS

INTRODUCTION

I N MY PRACTICE as an ophthalmologist, we say that the worst part of cataract surgery is the week before the actual procedure. That's when patients really start to think about the procedure and anticipate its effects. Many patients get concerned at this point about whether the surgery will hurt or whether they will lose their vision. And if they previously had a bad experience with some other procedure, they will be afraid of the cataract surgery.

These concerns and fears are very important and very real. A patient's attitude affects his ability to relax and cooperate with us during surgery so that we can do the best possible job. Therefore, it is essential that we help a patient understand the procedure, and that we provide as much comfort and reassurance as possible.

But for some people, it doesn't matter how much support we offer. Some patients are going to worry about all aspects of their lives. They're paralyzed by their worries, and they can't enjoy life.

The perspective of worry blinds us to the wonderful realities of God's loving care. We fail to be grateful for His sovereign rule in our lives. Too often we worry about things that are not so and we imagine situations that are not realities. One of the greatest reasons we worry is that we do not appreciate the Giver of life or the life that He gives us. Our lack of appreciation impairs our perspective and disposition more than we realize.

For example, when we are sick we worry about getting well, failing to realize that God has made our bodies with an estimated 60 trillion cells that are actively working to bring about healing. Our worry actually hinders that healing process. Our Creator's intelligent design in our DNA has gone before us to prepare the way for our healing. But too many times we are oblivious to His "ever-present help in trouble" (Ps. 46:1) because of our worry and lack of appreciation.

I often ask my patients if they have thanked God for their pancreas today. Probably not, but it has been working 24/7 for them since their birth. And there is much more that God is doing for them and will do for them. Yet, their mind-set of anxious worry shows a lack of trust in the Lord. It does not reflect a thankful spirit or appreciation of the Creator and all of His wisdom.

We understand medically that worry is self-destructive Yet, worry is unnecessary in the light of our faithful and sovereign Lord's care for His highest creation—mankind. Still, we all grapple with it and need to find help to overcome its deadly influence.

Do you know someone who has been paralyzed by fear and negative thinking? Or have you personally ever been so worried that you couldn't think clearly, couldn't sleep peacefully, or couldn't act wisely? This kind of chronic worry is a highly infectious disease that can permeate our inner being. It can infect our thoughts, attitudes, and actions. It can destroy us physically and emotionally. Worst of all, it can destroy us spiritually, because chronic worry drives a wedge between us and God. When we're ruled by worry, we don't have complete trust and faith in God. We don't think we can depend on Him. We feel isolated and alone. We blame God for all the bad circumstances in our lives, and we fail to see the blessings He provides.

The Treatment for Worry

Everyday, we must resist the temptation to worry and fear. I believe the most effective treatment for worry is two-fold: cultivating a spirit of thanksgiving and learning to appreciate the Creator, Redeemer, and Giver of life. When we learn to appreciate God's sovereignty and His faithfulness, our mind-set of worry is dislodged by trust in the power and love of God. And we learn to live in His peace.

I've seen this treatment work time and again in the lives of my patients. They have shown me that a constant attitude of thanksgiving breaks the grip of fear. These patients, in addition to facing their own surgery, may have family members who are dying; they may have financial problems; or they may be struggling in a personal relationship. They're certainly sad at times as they grapple with the problems in their lives, but they're not worried. They're thankful to God, and they continually seek His presence. They are thankful for all of the ways He provides for them, including their pending surgery, which they know will help them. Because of their faith, they can look beyond their struggles and see God at work. These thankful patients have the same concerns and problems many of us face, but they *choose* not to worry. They choose to be thankful.

A thankful spirit

Patients who "beat" worry have learned to live the words of the apostle Paul:

> Rejoice in the Lord always. I will say it again: Rejoice! Let your gentleness be evident to all. The Lord is near. *Do not be anxious* about anything, but in everything, by prayer and petition, with thanksgiving, present your requests to God. And the peace of God, which transcends all understanding, will guard your hearts and your minds in Christ Jesus.
> —PHILIPPIANS 4:4–7, *emphasis added*

Paul tells us that the thankful spirit is the proper mind-set for all believers. He tells us to not worry, but to always be thankful to the Lord. Just like my patients who demonstrate a mind-set of gratitude, we can reject worry. We can rejoice with thanksgiving. When we're focused on the Person of Jesus Christ in thanksgiving, our anxieties and fears can be wiped away. Our hearts can overflow with a spirit of peace and joy because He lives in us.

What a relief to know that each of us can turn to God and put our lives in His hands! We can be grateful for His blessings and let thanksgiving fill our hearts. We can be filled with peace regardless of our circumstances. We can be faithful to the One who faithfully provides. We must focus on Him with thankful hearts.

Appreciation

We have been taught that there are two categories of sin: sins of *commission*—what we do—and sins of *omission*—what we fail to do. My patients constantly hear me say that my greatest sin of commission is worry and my greatest sin of omission is failure to appreciate the Giver and the gift of life. *Appreciation* involves a sensitive awareness and an expression of admiration, approval, or gratitude. To *appreciate* means to place such high value on something or someone that it evokes our deep admiration.[1]

To truly appreciate the gift of life, we must first become aware of the Creator, the Giver of all life. Our eternal Creator designed life with a divine purpose. Learning to appreciate the Creator brings us into understanding of purpose. It brings into focus that purpose for our lives. As we learn to reverence and esteem our Creator-Redeemer, we are filled with thanksgiving for His benevolence, wisdom, majesty, and power already at work in our lives. We focus on His goodness and love, especially in dealing with the matters that cause anxiety.

Failure to properly appreciate God aborts the possibility of a thankful spirit. Without cultivating that divine relationship, we feel alone, isolated, and totally responsible for our own happiness and success in life. This sense of isolation traps us in self-centered, selfish mentalities, which are destructive in many aspects. They result in broken relationships, fear, insecurity, and many other unhealthy "syndromes."

Lack of appreciation for God, our Designer and Giver of life, will inevitably cause us to take all of life for granted. We fail to appreciate not only ours, but also the precious lives of those around us. Like all other sin, lack of gratitude brings with it terrible consequences, the most grave being a lack of relationship with God. Conversely, developing a personal relationship with God eliminates the destructive power of anxiety from our lives.

As we learn to appreciate the Creator and His design of all of life we will seek to know His wisdom rather than rely on our own confusion. We will look to his sovereignty, power, and gracious promises instead of our own frustrated perspective. When we learn to deeply admire and appreciate God, we quickly discover that God is much greater than all our problems. We become convinced that when we are worrying, we simply need to focus on God, who will put our anxieties to shame and silence them. It is not always easy to quiet a mind that is "all worked up." But when a fresh vision of God breaks through, the child of God is renewed in his or her soul. We receive new strength to rest in the Lord and enjoy His peace (see Isaiah 26:3).

Are you weighed down with worry? Are you filled with fear? There's refuge in the loving arms of God. He will break the bonds of worry. He will banish fear. We get His real and lasting peace when we turn to Him and say, "Thank You, Father, for always loving me. Thank You for the eternity that You offer to me through the Person of Jesus Christ, who died and rose again for me." When we turn to Him for redemption, no longer will we fear and worry. Jesus promises a life of peace for those who accept His salvation:

> Do not let your hearts be troubled. Trust in God; trust also in me…Peace I leave with you; my peace I give you. I do not give to you as the world gives. Do not let your hearts be troubled and do not be afraid.
>
> —JOHN 14:1, 27

Certainly none of us can avoid the situations and circumstances that can create worry and fear. But we can counteract the worry itself by cultivating a spirit of thanksgiving through humble appreciation for our Creator and Redeemer. When we begin to grasp God's greatness, majesty, sovereignty, loving control, and wise purposes, we learn to cast ourselves on His care.

As we do, we will see that God has given us many reminders of His precise and detailed attention for our good in all of His creation. This reassures us that God is already at work, not only in creation around us, but also in the fulfilling of His promises to us as His children. He is absolutely faithful to those who turn to Him. Therefore, He says to us, "Trust Me!"

In this book, we explore ways to build our trust in God, deepen our faith, practice a spirit of thanksgiving, increase our appreciation for God, and take practical steps to win the war against worry. The discussion questions at the end of each chapter are designed to help you examine the fears and worries in your life and look at ways you can strengthen your own relationship with God. You may also use the questions as part of a group study to help you talk about real issues within a Christian setting. The discussions also include additional Scripture verses to provide further insight.

In addition to a bibliography and a Scripture index, this book includes one additional appendix called "Putting Promises Into Action." God's Word, the Bible, is filled with promises about how He will take care of us. This index lists His promises about specific issues and circumstances. When one issue weighs you down, you can turn here to read His promises and use these verses in the fight against fear.

> Do not fear, for I am with you.
>
> —ISAIAH 41:10

The Bible tells us repeatedly, "Fear not." Many of those passages are followed by the words "I am with you." It is because God is with us that we do not need to fear. He will always be with His children. May we learn to trust fully in God with thanksgiving for His grace. He will destroy fear and worry! He will give us peace now and forever! Amen!

Chapter 1

THE WORRY DISEASE

I MAGINE THAT I got a new sports car. It is just perfect. I love the color and the model. And it comes with all kinds of electronic extras and gizmos. It is the fanciest car in the world. But there is one problem. The brake constantly locks on one wheel. Every time I accelerate, I spin around in circles.

While this isn't a true story, it does illustrate how worry affects us as human beings. Worry puts a brake on one of our wheels. We may be the sharpest sports car in the world, but we will only go around in circles if worry consumes us.

Let me confess that I've spent a few sleepless nights worrying about my job, my wife, and my children. I know some people who, when they worry, have trouble eating. Others shut themselves up in their offices or homes. In their isolation, worry strangles them. Worry takes its toll in many areas of our lives. Let's look at some of its damaging effects.

Intellect

I tell my patients that my greatest sin of commission is *worry* and my greatest sin of omission is *lack of appreciation*. It is easy to take all of life for granted, not stopping to appreciate the wonder of the human body, for example, that uses its estimated 60 trillion cells to serve us daily. There is so much that God is continually doing for us—and will do for us—that we simply do not *appreciate*. This lack of relationship with God creates a mind-set of anxious worry rather than trust in the Lord. The result is an unthankful spirit and a lack of appreciation of our Creator and all of His wisdom that He has bestowed on mankind—His highest creation.

When our thought processes are cluttered with worry, we can't have creative and energetic ideas. We produce sloppy and inaccurate work. We focus more on the pressure that deadlines create rather than on the quality of our work. And if we have trouble eating or sleeping, it becomes even more difficult to focus our minds. We can't process information and decide what's important, so we're disorganized. We can't decide which plans to follow, and we are unproductive. We're distracted; we jump from one task to another and never have a feeling of completion. We become indecisive; we fear making the wrong decision so much that we can't make any decisions. We can become workaholics, driven by worries about job or financial security.

When we live in worry and fear, we fail to consider the faithfulness of our God to all who call upon Him in time of need. And we do not understand that He is benevolently sovereign—Ruler over all: "The LORD has established His throne in the heavens; And His sovereignty rules over all" (Ps. 103:19, NASB). In our lack of appreciation for God, we fail to receive His infinite love and peace that He offers us freely.

Emotions

Our worries produce an uneasiness in us that causes us to be irritable and susceptible to panic attacks. "Where did we park the car at the mall?" "Where are my glasses?" "Where is that pen?" "Where did I put that bill which is due today?" We also can be depressed, negative, critical, judgmental, domineering, and controlling. We isolate ourselves and end up living lonely lives. We might be able to force others to be around us, but they don't do it willingly because we're no fun to be with. In addition, worry stifles our ability to reach out to others. We don't want to let our guard down and trust others, so worry locks us up in a life of isolation. We get involved with fewer and fewer people and groups. We have problems building genuine friendships.

When we live in constant worry, our emotions seem out of control, and we do not respond normally to everyday situations.

Health

Worry is a progressive disease that can ruin our lives and even kill us. Worry depletes us and has tangible effects on our health. It may even cause us to have hypertension. It sometimes destroys our ability to fight against diseases by decreasing our natural immunity. Our decreased immunity permits common colds to strike us, and, if our immune system breaks down further, worry may even permit us to be stricken by more serious diseases. Certainly anxiety is the basis of many psychiatric diseases and psychosomatic diseases. Charles Mayo, co-founder of the Mayo Clinic, pointed out how worry affects the body. It affects the circulatory system, the heart, the glands, and the nervous system, to name just a few. Mayo used to say that he never knew of anybody who died of overwork, but he did know people who died of worry.[1]

We can worry ourselves to death, but we can never worry ourselves into a longer, healthier, happier life—a thankful life focused on God.

In contrast, when we're filled with a spirit of thanksgiving, we are at peace with God. We have learned to appreciate our Creator-Redeemer, and our humble response is to express our gratitude for His loving presence in our lives. When we have His peace, we're at peace with ourselves and others. We're productive at work, accomplishing a great deal more, because we can focus on the task at hand. We can eat properly, rest properly, and heal properly. We learn to deeply appreciate those around us and enjoy harmonious relationships with our family and friends. We're able to love and serve others, forgive them, be thankful for them, encourage them, and appreciate them. Our lives are filled with thanksgiving.

The life of Dr. Earl Arnett Seamands (1891–1984), long-time missionary in South India, beautifully illustrates the power of serving others. In 1919, he left a successful career as an engineer and moved his family to India to serve as missionaries there. Living in a third world country during the early part of the twentieth century was a daunting task. They earned a meager one hundred dollars a month and endured a tremendous cultural shock. Not only were they without important items like a piano and a car, they were also forced to live without running water or indoor plumbing. Unable to make the difficult adjustment to this primitive lifestyle, Mrs. Seamands complained loudly and incessantly. So negative was the atmosphere she created in her home and for those around her that, surprisingly, even some of Mr. Seamands' Christian colleagues suggested to him that he would do well to divorce her.

But this godly man's patient response to their suggestion was, "I can divorce her as you suggest, but that would not be what the Lord would want me to do. I can separate myself from her and her complaining and continue to live the life I want to live, or, I can constantly pray for her and become an intercessor for her rather than being her accuser." In this attitude of humility, he decided to intercede for his wife and assist her rather than destroy their marriage. Dr. Seamands surmounted the challenges of life through this difficult time and became a stronger servant of God. As he continued to pray for his wife, she began to change positively and become more tolerant of their challenging lifestyle. As a result, their family was blessed with two sons who have distinguished themselves in Christian ministry as well.[2]

As Mr. Seamands aligned himself with the will of God and allowed his love for his wife to keep him interceding for her, he overcame her critical attitudes and continual bickering. He served her in love and won over all odds to save his marriage and strengthen his ministry.

Mr. Seamands had a deep appreciation for God and desired to serve Him with a thankful spirit for His goodness and faithfulness. It was that focused priority that helped him to appreciate his wife, even though she was behaving in an unlovely manner.

His alignment with God gave him strength to overcome the negative situation in his home.

The chart on pages six and seven uses God's Word to show the difference between the mind-set of worry and the mind-set of peace and thanksgiving.

Chronic worry creates destructive anxiety and stress in our lives. It destroys our relationship with God and other people. When we embrace the negative mind-set of worry, we accuse others, judge others, discourage others, and try to control others. We're negative people who don't feel God's love and can't love others. But when we have a thankful spirit, God's peace and love fill our lives. Our focus is on His eternal presence and blessings. We are positive, trusting, loving, supportive, and appreciative. When we are thankful, positive people, it means we have learned to truly appreciate God, our Father, Savior, Provider, and Friend.

The attitudes of two sisters named Mary and Martha illustrate the difference between persons who worry and those who don't. Jesus and His disciples stopped at the sisters' house to visit and eat. While Martha scurried around the house getting everything ready for the meal, Mary sat at Jesus' feet and listened to Him talk. Finally, Martha was so irritated about doing all the work by herself that she complained to Jesus. "Lord, don't You care that my sister has left me to do the work by myself? Tell her to help me!" Jesus' words probably surprised her: Martha, Martha...you are worried and upset about many things, but only one thing is needed. Mary has chosen what is better, and it will not be taken away from her" (Luke 10:40–42).

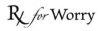

Worry	Thanksgiving
But the worries of this life, the deceitfulness of wealth and the desires for other things come in and choke the word, making it unfruitful. —MARK 4:19 *(Worry keeps us from listening to God.)*	I will listen to what God the LORD will say; he promises peace to his people. —PSALM 85:8 *(We listen to God.)*
If you keep on biting and devouring each other, watch out or you will be destroyed by each other. —GALATIANS 5:15 *(Worry causes poor relationships.)*	Let the peace of Christ rule in your hearts, since as members of one body you were called to peace. And be thankful. —COLOSSIANS 3:15 *(We have peaceful relationships.)*
The way of peace they do not know. —ROMANS 3:17 *(Worry destroys peace.)*	You will keep in perfect peace him whose mind is steadfast, because he trusts in you. —ISAIAH 26:3 *(We have internal peace.)*
Cursed is the one who trusts in man…He will be like a bush in the wastelands. —JEREMIAH 17:5–6 *(Worry dries us up spiritually.)*	The eternal God is your refuge, and underneath are the everlasting arms. —DEUTERONOMY 33:27 *(We feel God's provision.)*
The seed that fell among thorns stands for those who hear, but as they go on their way they are choked by life's worries…and they do not mature. —LUKE 8:14 *(Worry makes us unproductive in our work for the Lord and otherwise.)*	Trust in the LORD with all your heart and lean not on your own understanding; in all your ways acknowledge him, and he will make your paths straight. —PROVERBS 3:5–6 *(We are productive under God's guidance.)*

Worry	Thanksgiving
"Martha, Martha," the Lord answered, "you are worried and upset about many things." —LUKE 10:41 *(We are frazzled in our work.)*	Trust in the LORD…Delight yourself in the LORD…Commit your way to the LORD…Be still before the LORD and wait patiently for him. —PSALM 37:3–5, 7 *(We have peace in our work.)*
Do not love the world or anything in the world…The world and its desires pass away, but the man who does the will of God lives forever. —1 JOHN 2:15, 17 *(We're focused on the material world.)*	Though outwardly we are wasting away, yet inwardly we are being renewed day by day. —2 CORINTHIANS 4:16 *(We're focused on eternity.)*
Their father Jacob said to them, "You have deprived me of my children. Joseph is no more and Simeon is no more, and now you want to take Benjamin. Everything is against me!" —GENESIS 42:36 *(We miss God's purpose.)*	And we know that in all things God works for the good of those who love him, who have been called according to his purpose. —ROMANS 8:28 *(We know God is in control.)*
I have no refuge; no one cares for my life. —PSALM 142:4 *(We feel alone and isolated. We don't sense God's presence.)*	So do not fear, for I am with you; do not be dismayed, for I am your God. —ISAIAH 41:10 *(God is with us.)*

The problem wasn't that Martha was working. The problem was her attitude. Martha wasn't thankful that the Lord had come to visit with her. She did not appreciate His presence in the way her sister, Mary, did. Martha was worried about the burden His visit created—fixing a meal, preparing the house, tending to the guests. Jesus tried to show her that she needed to change her focus. Rather than giving priority to her work, she needed to give priority to the presence of God. Jesus praised Mary for her attitude. She knew the most important thing wasn't what she did. It was that she was thankful for the presence of the Lord and was aligned with Him. She esteemed Him for who He was and desired to sit at His feet in humility to listen to the words of the Master.

It's the same with each of us. Jesus sees through our work and worry. He knows that what we really need is to change our focus—from anxious activity to reverent relationship. We need to humble ourselves in His presence instead of pridefully trying to "make it" on our own. When we give priority only to our tangible actions and results, such as our work-related activities, without pursuing relationship with our Lord, we'll be filled with anxieties and fears. But when we're aligned with Him, those worries vanish. We're filled with thanksgiving for His presence in our lives. We see the way He guides our lives and blesses us. We're totally committed to Him. As a result, we're engulfed with the presence of God through the Person of Jesus Christ, who has promised to give us peace and rest:

> Come to me, all you who are weary and burdened, and I will give you rest. Take my yoke upon you and learn from me, for I am gentle and humble in heart, and you will find rest for your souls. For my yoke is easy and my burden is light.
> —MATTHEW 11:28–30

Which lifestyle would you choose? Would you rather pursue the God of peace or be paralyzed by worry?

The right choice seems clear, but it isn't always easy. Worry can sneak up on us. Satan knows that, given the choice, we'd rather have peace than the turmoil that worry creates. So he uses our own weak human will and desires to lure us into a lifestyle of worry. Worry starts innocently enough, I think, as a normal, natural concern about our basic needs. Do we have enough money to buy adequate food, clothes, and shelter? Is our health good? Are our friends and family healthy and happy?

It is perfectly natural to have these concerns. In fact, it's good that we are concerned, because then we're moved to proper action. We work so we can afford food, clothes, and shelter. We go to the doctor when we don't feel well. We try to be loving and thoughtful to our family and friends. And we appreciate God, expressing gratitude for all He provides.

But Satan uses the values of the world—tangible goods we can see, hold, and measure—to lure us away from our trust in God. As we become less God-centered and more self-centered, our natural concerns become worries. We quit trusting that God will provide adequate food and clothes. We believe that we have to focus on meeting our own needs for the right clothes, the right house, the right car, the right job, the right spouse, and the right country club. We think we have to take care of ourselves and we worry about circumstances and events beyond our control. We can become more and more selfish, and then we don't trust others because we assume they're selfish also. We worry about irrelevant and inconsequential concerns, such as whether there's enough money in the parking meter. We're overcome with nega-tive thoughts and can't tell the difference between legitimate concerns and problems that exist only in our heads.

Worry has us firmly in its grip. It has happened to all of us at some point in our lives. None of us is immune to selfishness and the worry that it creates.

> We all, like sheep, have gone astray, each of us has turned
> to his own way; and the LORD has laid on him the iniquity
> of us all.
> —ISAIAH 53:6

This verse is a great motivation for me. First, I see myself going my own way, acting on my own dreams, aspirations, and desires. Then, I see Christ on the cross, bearing my sins. In the first scene, I'm enjoying my sinful pleasure and not caring about

God. In the other scene, Christ is caring about me and bearing the penalty for my sins.

Two effects result from my visualization of this verse. First, it breaks my heart and challenges me. Second, it provides strength of motivation to know that He loves me to that degree. It binds my heart to Him so much that I want to be loyal to Him. I begin again to trust in God with renewed strength and put aside my selfish ways in order to seek His will.

Will you do that with me now? Pray with me:

> *Lord, I am selfish. I have sought my own way and ignored You. Forgive me when I try to live by worldly standards. Forgive me for thinking that I can't depend on You. I commit myself again to seeking Your will and not the ways of the world. I know that I am Your child and that You will take care of me. Thank You for Your endless fountains of love, mercy, and grace. Thank You for the strength that comes from trusting in You. Amen.*

There's good news for us sinners. Worry isn't permanent! In the next few chapters, we'll look more closely at the forms selfishness takes and the different ways it creates worry. We'll also see God's plan for combating selfishness and surrendering to His will. And we will understand how meditating on the wonders of God's creation all around us can evoke deep appreciation and strengthen our trust in God.

Discussion Questions

1. What are you worried about now? How is it affecting your health? How is it affecting your relationships?

   _____

   _____

   _____

2. What makes you feel peaceful? How does that attitude affect your health and relationships?

   _____

   _____

   _____

3. How can you deepen your appreciation for God and for His gracious gift of life?

   _____

   _____

   _____

4. List some ways to practice being thankful this week. For example, say "thank you" to someone you encounter today—a sales clerk, a receptionist, or a neighbor. Or write a note to someone special.

   _____

   _____

   _____

   _____

5. What are some of your obstacles to asking God for
   His peace?

   _____

   _____

   _____

6. What Scripture speaks to your heart about your
   worries?

   _____

   _____

   _____

For further reflection

Search me, O God, and know my heart; test me and know
my anxious thoughts. See if there is any offensive way in
me, and lead me in the way everlasting.

—PSALM 139:23–24

The writer of this psalm is asking for true intimacy with God.
Ask God to explore your own heart and help you wipe away any
anxious thoughts that might be there.

Chapter 2

AWE, APPRECIATION,
and ADORATION

THE SPIRIT AND practice of thanksgiving is a powerful weapon against the self-destructive "vice" of worry—a vice into which we are all too prone to fall. Why are we so vulnerable to worry? Lack of appreciation for the Creator and His sovereign, benevolent rule over all creation is a major reason for the insecurity, fear, and worry that many suffer continually. Many people fail to live a life of thanksgiving because they do not truly appreciate the gift of life they have been given. When we fail to appreciate God, it follows that we do not appreciate His gift of life to us—and to others.

As a result, we are doomed to living selfish lives, seeking only to please ourselves, which causes us to make unfair demands on others. In our self-centered blindness, we think our security, our happiness, and our well-being depends on us alone. Anxiety and worry plague the heart and mind that cannot control circumstances and people to secure its perceived "happiness." Without a revelation of God's great power and love, we can never learn to truly appreciate the gift of life that God has graciously given us to enjoy. In her book, *Radical Gratitude*, Ellen Vaughn comments on this sad reality:

> We live in a land that has largely lost a sense of holy reverence, let alone the transcendent. Most everything is assessed by the criterion, "How does it affect me?" In a supremely self-referential culture it's hard to conceive of anything that is so wholly Other...Far too often we trivialize the holy, perceiving God as an extension of ourselves. God is white, just like us. Or black, or Asian, or Hispanic,

or whatever…No. God is huge. Mysterious. Multidimensional.[1]

It is a habit of grateful people, Vaughn concludes, to "look up and see God as God. When we look up to Him, we are first overwhelmed and awed, then full of gratitude that One so huge would deign to love ones so small."[2] Gratitude to God serves as a catalyst to greater appreciation for the gift of life He has given us.

Appreciation, simply defined, means "to grasp the worth and value of something or someone; to esteem and properly revere them." I am convinced that if we pause to appreciate God's creation we see all around us, our selfish perspective of life can be changed. The Scriptures confirm that we can see God in His creation: "For since the creation of the world God's invisible qualities…have been clearly seen, being understood from what has been made, so that men are without excuse" (Rom. 1:20).

As we allow our hearts to be filled with awe for the miraculous handiwork that we are as human beings, we begin to bow in gratitude for God's great kindness to us. We become aware of His great faithfulness and learn to rest in His sovereign rule over our lives. That is how true appreciation for God and His creation can rid us of our worry and anxiety. Instead of our complaining and negative attitudes, appreciation for God leads our hearts to the spontaneous response of *adoration*, filling us with praise and thanksgiving for His gift of life—now and for eternity.

We need to take time to appreciate the world around us and to allow the wonders of creation to fill us with awe. Knowledge of the creation reveals to us the nature of our Creator. As we behold the Creator's infinite hand in our universe, we begin to understand that He is outside of time or any other finite, limiting force. He is eternal. And if He designed life with a divine purpose, He must desire to reveal His eternal purpose to our hearts.

Jesus prayed to the Father that He would give eternal life to all He had given Him. "Now this is eternal life: that they may know you, the only true God, and Jesus Christ, whom you have sent"

(John 17:3). Learning to appreciate the Creator can be a beginning point to unlocking for us the eternal benefits of knowing God, receiving His Son, Jesus Christ, as our Savior, and thereby experiencing the infinite quality of life that is eternal.

Yet, it has been my observation that even people of faith, born-again believers in Christ, who love their Creator-Redeemer, often lack appreciation for His creation. Their complaining hearts fail to comprehend the wondrous gift of beauty in nature. And often they abuse the gift of physical health He has given them. Their lack of appreciation for their Creator keeps them from fully enjoying that quality of eternal life they have been given in this life.

Surrendering our lives to our awesome Creator–Redeemer allows us to enter into divine purpose for our lives. As we express our gratitude to God, our hearts are humbled and filled with appreciation. The disease of worry is suffocated and displaced when a believer's heart is filled with adoration and worship of God. The psalmist demonstrates how our humble adoration for God brings the deepest satisfaction a human heart can know:

> O LORD, how many are Your works! In wisdom You have
> made them all; The earth is full of Your possessions...
> I will sing to the LORD as long as I live; I will sing praise
> to my God while I have my being. Let my meditation be
> pleasing to Him...I shall be glad in the LORD.
> —PSALM 104:24, 33–34, NASB

Do you have a special place in nature where you love to breathe deeply and meld your psyche with the view of God's creation in which you are reveling? Do you love to look with awe into a darkened sky, filled with billions of tiny sparkling lights? Do you enjoy the awesome power of a thunderstorm with its lightning flashes and loud crashes? Perhaps you are fascinated by a brilliantly colored wild flower blooming under a rocky crag where no one else will even see it. You probably have a favorite nature scene or sound that fills your heart with awe, if only for a moment. The phenomena of nature's wonders seem infinite in number and are exquisite in beauty, filling the observant heart with appreciation.

If you do not feel thankful, I suggest that you meditate on the greatness of God in creation and consider the words of the psalmist: "The earth is full of Your possessions." Let your eyes see His creation; let your ears hear the sounds of it; enjoy its fragrance and its touch. Let your spirit be enlarged and refreshed by the exquisite beauty surrounding you during your ordinary day. You can become filled with awe and wonder as you behold with new eyes the handiwork of your Creator. And you will learn to express adoration and praise to God for who He is and who He has made you to be in His great purposes.

> Know that the LORD is God. It is he who made us, and we are his; we are his people, the sheep of his pasture. Enter his gates with thanksgiving and his courts with praise; give thanks to him and praise his name.
>
> —PSALM 100:3–4

Adoration for God brings the grateful heart into deep intimacy with its Creator-Redeemer. God responds to our love expression with the depths of His love—"God is love" (1 John. 4:8). Only that divine love relationship can truly satisfy the human heart's cry for peace, rest, security, and fulfillment. Again, the psalmist expresses the wonder of belonging to God and of knowing the peace and security of His tender care:

> The LORD is my shepherd, I shall not be in want. He makes me lie down in green pastures, he leads me beside quiet waters, he restores my soul. He guides me in paths of righteousness for his name's sake. Even though I walk through the valley of the shadow of death, I will fear no evil, for you are with me; your rod and your staff, they comfort me.
>
> —PSALM 23:1–4

When you are willing to quit looking for security and satisfaction in circumstances or people, and begin to allow awe and appreciation for the Creator-Redeemer to fill your heart, you will find your life filled with adoration for Him. And you will know deep within your heart that you have no reason to worry or fret as you continually discover God's unfathomable, eternal love filling your life.

Discussion Questions

1. Do you have a favorite "nature spot"? Does it evoke awe of the Creator in your mind and heart? Describe it and the feeling it gives you.

_____

_____

_____

2. Have you compared the infinite greatness of the Creator, God, to your finiteness? Can you trust His love to have control of your life? What areas of your life do you need to relinquish to His infinite love?

_____

_____

_____

3. What divine attribute of God do you appreciate most? Does that characteristic of God evoke adoration from your heart? If so, how do you express your deep love to Him?

_____

_____

4. If you have not done so, memorize Psalm 23 this
   week. If you have, recite it prayerfully each day
   and consider the beautiful picture of God's peace,
   security, and love that it reveals for those who have
   relinquished their lives to the Great Shepherd.

For further reflection

Jesus said:

> But seek first his kingdom and his righteousness, and all
> these things will be given to you as well. Therefore do not
> worry about tomorrow, for tomorrow will worry about
> itself.
>
> —MATTHEW 6:33–34

When we make God the priority in our life, He promises to
resolve our other needs. Discuss how this truth could be better
applied in your life.

Chapter 3

REALITY vs. WORRY

REALITY IS DEFINED as the "quality or state of being real."[1] It is a fact that many of the things we worry about simply are not real. They are based on "what ifs?" And even the things we worry about that appear to be real may not be when considered in light of the higher spiritual reality that God offers us. For example, we may feel alone, unloved, and without worth. But if we look to the reality of God's Word, we would know that those feelings do not correspond with true reality for believers who have put their trust in God:

> God has said, "Never will I leave you; never will I forsake you."
>
> —HEBREWS 13.5

> God is love… We love because he first loved us.
>
> —1 JOHN 4:16, 19

Our great Creator, God, has infinite love for His creation. He has designed us to live in peace, love, joy, and deep satisfaction in relationship with Him. If we were aligned with God's reality it would be impossible to embrace worry, which is based in fear. His Word promises, "Perfect love drives out fear" (1 John 4:18).

To help us align ourselves with God's reality, let's consider a few marvels of God's handiwork as observed by modern science. From the precise parameters of our planet to the faultless functioning of our human DNA, we can learn to appreciate God's power and love revealed in His creation. The grandeur of creation's scientific realities can evoke awe and appreciation in our hearts for God.

We can face down our worries by meditating on the wonder

of God's power and His sovereign care for all of creation—especially His love for mankind whom He made in His own image. We begin to understand that God is at work on our behalf, just as thoroughly, precisely, powerfully, and caringly as He is in the universe. And we learn to rest in the sovereignty of our great Creator–Redeemer.

Dr. Richard Swenson is an award-winning educator and best-selling author. In 2003, the Christian Medical and Dental Associations honored him with the Educator of the Year award. He has traveled to over fifty countries for purposes of speaking, practice, or study and has presented to such prestigious groups as the Mayo Clinic, members of the United Nations, the Pentagon, and members of Congress. Dr. Swenson says: "The more we understand about God's power, the less we worry about our weakness."[2] And because God is love (1 John 4:8), we can trust His power to meet our every need. In short, when we focus on God we learn that we have no need to worry. As you consider some scientific facts about life as we know it, allow your heart to experience awe and gratitude for the gift of life.

In his book, *More Than Meets the Eye* (also presented in a fascinating DVD series), Dr. Swenson describes the human body as a "reflection of the brilliance, the genius, the power, the precision, the sophistication of an almighty Creator. There are 10 to the 28th (10 with 28 zeros) atoms in the human body—more than there are stars in the universe. We turn over a trillion atoms every 1/ billionth of a second. And, if we examine the subatomic space where the smaller-than-atom particles such as electrons, protons, and neutrons dwell, we find we are perhaps infinite in a subatomic direction. The scientific theory of 'super strings' (fundamental constituents of subatomic reality represented as strings of energy as opposed to particles) postulates that the most basic building blocks of life lurking in the microscopic sphere of our body are a 100 million billion times smaller than a proton particle."[3] Consider the greatness of God's handiwork in creating the human body, which scientists today are only beginning to understand.

The heart beats two and a half billion times in a lifetime and pumps blood over 60 thousand miles of blood vessels. We make 2 million red blood cells every second. Put side-by-side, they would circle the earth at the equator four times. In our lungs at any given moment we have 150 million air molecules. What the retina of the eye does every 1/3 of a second would take a supercomputer 100 years to do. The ear has a million moving parts and in many ways is even more sensitive than the eye. The human brain, at a mere three pounds, is the most complex and orderly arrangement of matter in the universe. The brain stores the equivalent of 25 million books. And it can function at ten thousand trillion computations per second.[4]

Perhaps the most amazing fact of human life is the human genome and the DNA. There are an estimated 60 trillion cells in the human body and each cell has DNA in its chromosomes. The DNA in one cell is 6 feet long. If we stretched out all the DNA from one human body, it would reach 100 billion miles. Yet, the initial single-cell DNA of every human being alive today—all six billion—weighed together would total 1/1,000[th] of an ounce. Science reveals the power, precision, and sovereignty of God—He is impressive. So, why do we live in such a stupor, being insecure and anxious? We forget who God is; we fail to trust. It is not that He has failed to demonstrate or teach us, but that we have failed to understand. We are dim. We should ask Him to take the dimness of our soul away.[5]

These marvels of scientific reality help us to understand our own finiteness and should inspire our hearts to bow before an infinite Creator. Dr. Swenson comments: "Do we have any idea the level of power and precision we are witnessing here? What we need is a new vision of God—the real God—not some vague image…the kind of God who stuns the physicists with symmetry; the mathematicians with precision; the engineers with design; the politicians with power; and the poets with beauty. Don't fear science; God invented it all. And a clear understanding of what He has done only enhances our view of Him."[6]

The psalmist understood this intimate relationship of God with mankind:

> For you created my inmost being; you knit me together in my mother's womb. I praise you because I am fearfully and wonderfully made; your works are wonderful, I know that full well. My frame was not hidden from you when I was made in the secret place. When I was woven together in the depths of the earth, your eyes saw my unformed body. All the days ordained for me were written in your book before one of them came to be.
>
> —PSALM 139:13–16

Dr. Swenson wryly confesses that he asks himself two questions when he arises each morning. First, he asks, "Is God worried?" If the answer to that question is yes, he cancels his agenda for the day because it is all over. If God is worried, we are doomed. But if the answer to the first question is no, then he asks himself the second question: "Then why am I worried?" A greater vision of God's sovereignty and faithfulness will let us see the world from God's view and dispel our anxieties.[7]

Our Creator, God, is continually acting according to His eternal purposes for mankind, for the nations, and for each individual life. As we choose to align ourselves with that divine purpose, we come under His divine protection. We experience His great faithfulness to guide us through all of life's changing situations.

Christ came to earth to sacrifice His life for all of mankind, making it possible to become realigned with God. When we accept Christ as our Savior and surrender continually to His will for our lives, we have peace with God. When we focus on His loving, eternal plan for our lives, we find ourselves being continually released from deeper levels of anxiety and worry. We learn to appreciate God and to trust our lives to Him, resting in His great redemption. The Scriptures teach clearly that as believers we are not to entertain worry and fear. The apostle Paul taught believers:

> Rejoice in the Lord always. I will say it again: Rejoice!…Do not be anxious about anything, but in everything, by prayer and petition, with thanksgiving, present your requests to God. And the peace of God, which transcends all understanding, will guard your hearts and your minds in Christ Jesus.
>
> —PHILIPPIANS 4:4, 6–7

And Jesus comforted His disciples and instructed them:

> Peace I leave with you; my peace I give you. I do not give to you as the world gives. Do not let your hearts be troubled and do not be afraid.
>
> —JOHN 14:27

Understanding the scientific realities involved in God's creation to give to us the gift of life should put to rest any doubt of His great love for us. He created mankind in His image and desires that we enjoy intimate relationship with Him and bring glory and honor to His great name. As stated in the Westminster Catechism, "Man's chief end is to glorify God, and to enjoy him forever."[8]

Eternity spent with God will be filled with the wonder of who He is—getting to know Him and His wonderful works. Yet, even now, if we seek it in faith, our daily lives will be impacted with the sovereign power, majesty, and love of God, causing us to relinquish all fear, doubt, and anxious worry. And we will be filled with gratitude and thanksgiving, bowing our hearts before Him in worship and awe for His infinite attention to the details of our lives.

Discussion Questions

1. In what areas of your life does your sense of "reality" need to be redefined to reflect God's spiritual reality (His Word and promises)?

_____

_____

_____

_____

_____

2. How would accepting God's spiritual reality in those areas of your life change your perspective?...your attitudes?...your actions?

_____

_____

_____

_____

_____

3. Have you considered the scientific wonder that your human body is? How could you bring greater glory to God in your body? Some examples would be exercising, eating, and giving up destructive habits.

_____

_____

_____

_____

4. What specific steps could you take to align yourself with God's spiritual reality to displace areas of
worry in your life?

_____

_____

_____

_____

_____

For further reflection

Read Psalm 139 aloud as if you were praying it yourself. Allow
the spiritual reality of God's intimate love to flood over your
mind and heart as you declare His care for you in the words of
the psalmist.

Chapter 4

REALITY in the COSMOS

I N CONSIDERING THE reality of God's sovereign love and power in the previous chapter, we observed briefly the marvelous miracle of the human body. We can also observe the reality of God by peering into the heavens to discover His exquisite handiwork there. According to the Scriptures, God simply decreed into existence every galaxy and star:

> And God said, "Let there be lights in the expanse of the sky to separate the day from the night, and let them serve as signs to mark seasons and days and years, and let them be lights in the expanse of the sky to give light on the earth." And it was so. God made two great lights—the greater light to govern the day and the lesser light to govern the night. He also made the stars.
>
> —GENESIS 1:14–16

Scientists marvel at the astounding facts they have discovered as they probe the beauty of God's cosmos. Our universe contains an estimated 100 billion galaxies, and each galaxy contains an estimated 100 billion stars. There were over 100 parameters that had to be precisely exact for life to exist on planet Earth. Life does exist—created and sustained by God. Today, there are almost six and a half billion people alive on our planet. Our cultures vary, but we share the same miracle—life. A clear, scientific understanding of what God has done only enhances our view of Him. His precision is impressive; His sovereignty is on display. How can such power fail to dominate our every thought and action, to rescue us from our everyday insecurities? It is not that God has failed to demonstrate His nature; it is just that we are slow to understand. What we need is a new vision of God—the real God. He is brilliant and wise, powerful, precise, yet also compassionate, intimate, and personal.[1]

Scientists studying the handiwork of God have discovered that the mass of the universe is 10^{50} (10 followed by 50 zeros) tons. To convert that mass to pure energy we would multiply it by the speed of light, squared. The result is a fantastically large number. There are 10^{79} elementary particles in the universe, counting neutrons, protons, and quarks. Yet, though scientists have been able to identify and calculate the mass and energy of this gigantic universe, *they have not been able to reproduce or create one ounce of mass or energy.* The first law of thermo-dynamics (represented by Albert Einstein's famous equation, $E = MC^2$) states that energy or mass cannot be created—or destroyed. Remember, the entire universe came into existence when God spoke. And God knows where every particle is at every moment because He is omniscient—all knowing. He doesn't try to know; He just knows because of the essence of who He is—an all-knowing God.[2]

God's omniscience alone should infuse believers with awe and wonder, evoking our trust and surrender to the lordship of Christ. Considering this divine attribute of an all-knowing God helps us to understand why Jesus could say, "Indeed, the very hairs of your head are all numbered. Don't be afraid" (Luke 12:7).

The level of precision of the universe is 10^{10} to the 27th, a number that is humanly impossible to describe. The minute details of every movement of the stars, every element of the planets, every formative attribute of the earth are precisely what is needed to sustain life, to the unfathomable degree that the most brilliant scientist could never begin to reproduce. The sheer magnitude of the universe that has been discovered to date is beyond our comprehension.[3]

There are an estimated 100 billion galaxies in the universe. Many are irregular, without any shape. Our Milky Way galaxy is a spiral shape, flat like a pancake, with a center black hole. It is spinning at a half million miles an hour. The planet, Venus, is the size of the earth. But it has very long days because it takes

8 months to rotate one time. And it is the only planet that is retrograde—it rotates in the opposite direction of all the others in our galaxy. As a result, its atmospheric pressure is 90 times greater than the earth's. The upper clouds of Venus drip sulfuric acid, and there are surface hurricane winds constantly, along with deafening thunder and lightning strikes, and a 1,000 degree Fahrenheit surface temperature.[4]

Jupiter, the largest planet in our galaxy, could hold one thousand earths. It rotates so fast that one day is only 8 hours long. It has surface winds of 1,000 miles per hour. While it cannot sustain any known form of life, it performs a very important role for our earth. If Jupiter were not placed precisely where it is, comets would strike the earth 1,000 times more frequently than they do, threatening our very existence. Saturn is the beauty queen of the Milky Way's planets. Its gigantic rings are exquisite to behold. It contains 750 times the volume of the earth. Two of its moons perform an extraordinary feat. Every four years they shift in their orbits, looking as though they are about to crash into each other. But then, at the last "moment" they do a kind of "dance"—and switch orbits.[5]

Yet for all the beauty and fascinating aspects of the other planets, Earth is the only known inhabitable planet. The precision of over 100 parameters that had to be exactly, mathematically defined to seemingly impossible limits in order to sustain life as we know it, include these: Not too much mass, not too little; not too close to the sun, not too far away; not too close to Jupiter, not too far away. The gravitational force had to be precise; the number of stars had to be precise; the moon had to be just the right size and in the right place, etc. In 1687 Isaac Newton wrote in his book, *Principia*, (still touted as one of the most important works in physics), "Thus God arranged planets at distances from the sun."[6]

Robin Collins, PhD, is a highly influential professor of physics and philosophy who served as postdoctoral fellow at Northwestern University. Years of research have resulted in numerous books, including *The Well-Tempered Universe: God, Fine-Tuning, and the Laws of Nature.* Collins explains: "When scientists talk about the fine-tuning of the universe they are generally referring to the extraordinary balancing of the fundamental laws and parameters of physics and the initial conditions of the universe. Our minds can't comprehend the precision of some of them. The result is a universe that has just the right conditions to sustain life. The coincidences are simply too amazing to have been the result of happenstance—as Paul Davies said, 'the impression of design is overwhelming.'"[7]

These great scientific minds attest to the power of God that set the universe in motion and watches over it with just as much care as when He created it. He is as involved in our personal "universe" of troubles and cares, plans and desires, hopes and dreams as He is in the cosmos. As we seek to know Him and align ourselves with His sovereign plan for our lives, we can live in peace and freedom from all anxiety and fear.

Allan R. Sandage, renowned astronomer who was assistant to Edwin Hubble and then became his successor, has for half a century been a leader in our observational quest to understand the stars, galaxies, and the universe. Sandage has quantified the expansion of the universe in many important ways and was the first to recognize the existence of quasars without strong radio emission, leading the way to discovery of some of the most distant objects in the universe. He developed new observational techniques and opened new areas of inquiry in fields ranging from the pulsations of stars to tests of cosmological models at great distances, to searches for quasars. When receiving the 2000 Cosmology Prize, it was stated that his lifetime contribution to extragalactic astronomy and cosmology, and his influence on his colleagues, is unmatched by any other astronomer.[8]

Dr. Sandage began his scientific journey as an atheist. He later confessed that "it was my science that drove me to the conclusion that the world is much more complicated than can be explained by science. We can't understand the universe in any clear way without the supernatural."[9] He recognized the sovereign power of the Creator that could not be matched, or even understood, by the finiteness of man's mind. Dr. Sandage found that in understanding the reality of the supernatural power of God revealed in the universe, and seeking to become acquainted with His divine essence—which is love (1 John 4:19)—we can be delivered from all unbelief, fear, worry, and insecurity.

All of creation sings of the wonders of God's power and love. And the stars are seemingly the centerpiece of the heavens. The Old Testament prophet declared:

> Lift your eyes and look to the heavens: Who created all these? He who brings out the starry host one by one, and calls them each by name. Because of his great power and mighty strength, not one of them is missing.
>
> —ISAIAH 40: 26

It is estimated that there are between 10^{20} and 10^{24} stars in the universe. All stars are hydrogen bombs, generating continual light and extreme heat. A *neutron star* is a small star, by comparison, but very dense in mass. A spoonful of a neutron star would weigh 100 million tons. *Pulsars* are neutron stars that can rotate 100 times a second and emit radio waves. *Gamma ray bursts*, while they are not stars, deserve to be mentioned with these phenomenal extravaganzas of the night skies. They emit the most energetic form of electromagnetic radiation. Some gamma ray bursts are as bright as the rest of the universe combined. The surface of our sun converts 4 million tons of the mass of its surface into energy every second. That heat energy screams across the solar system, in the form of photons, and we receive 1 billionth of it to warm the earth. So much heat energy is produced by our sun that if a pin head were heated to the core temperature of the sun and brought to earth, it would kill everyone within 1,000 miles around. Recently, the sun shot out a solar flare, which floated as a giant magnetic cloud, 30 million miles in diameter and moving at a million miles an hour.[10]

31

All the heavens demonstrate the reality of God in the cosmos. While these cosmic phenomena stagger our finite minds, we should be comforted to know that if God gives this much attention to the details of His creation, we can be assured that He is working in the details of our lives. We can bring to Him the cares that cause us worry. As we exchange the "pretend" realities seen through the eyes of worry for the true reality of our sovereign God who loves us, we will enter into peace and rest in His redemption. As the psalmist declared:

> How precious to me are your thoughts, O God! How vast is the sum of them! Were I to count them, they would outnumber the grains of sand. When I awake, I am still with you.
>
> —PSALM 139:17–18

Dr. Swenson explains the existence of the carbon atom as an example of seemingly impossible odds for life as we know it. One Christian chemist called the carbon atom "God's autograph." Carbon is the fourth most common element in the universe and all of life that we have discovered is carbon-based. It is the only element that has the properties needed for supporting the richness of life as we know it. Using hydrogen, oxygen, nitrogen, and other elements, it can form an infinite number of compounds. Scientists have measured over one million existing carbon compounds. Many thousands of these are vital to life processes. Carbon is unique among all of the elements; no other element can form the chemical bonds in carbon.

Yet, the formation of the carbon element is so unlikely that it should not be able to exist. Consider this simplified explanation of its formation. To form a carbon atom requires first that 2 hydrogen come together to form a *helium*. Then two helium come together and form a *beryllium*. This beryllium compound is very unstable—it lasts only for a billionth of a billionth of a second. In that tiny fraction of time, in order for a carbon atom to form, another helium needs to attach itself to the unstable beryllium. And it can't be just any helium in the area. The nuclear energy levels, or *resonance*, of the helium needed to attach to the beryllium must be precisely matched in order to form one carbon atom. Imagine all the carbon atoms required to form the basis of all of life as we know it meeting those exacting requirements for each of their formation.[11]

Fred Hoyle, brilliant British astrophysicist and a self-proclaimed atheist, predicted this "resonance number" for the "matching" helium and beryllium needed to form a carbon atom. Then he asked scientists at Cal Tech to scientifically calculate the number. They worked for a week with their computers to calculate the resonance number needed to form a carbon element. They discovered that the number Hoyle had predicted was the exact number that they calculated. This discovery shook Hoyle's atheistic world-view to the core. He said, "A common sense interpretation of the facts suggests that a super-intellect has monkeyed with the physics as well as the chemistry and the biology."[12]

Appreciating the "impossible," minute details of exquisite design required to form the basic building blocks of life should help us to rest in the omniscient, loving care of our Creator-Redeemer. As we choose to bow in humility before this unfathomable Creator, God, casting our care on Him, we realize how much He cares for us. The Scriptures clearly teach: "Cast all your anxiety on him because he cares for you" (1 Pet. 5:7). Dr. Swenson sums up our confidence in God:

> The sovereignty, power, design, genius, majesty, precision, caring, and intimacy of an almighty God takes away our fear, removes our frustration, and allows us to trust Him with the running of the universe. It allows us to…seek His will not our own, and take our role instead of trying to have His role. To know Him is to trust Him and to trust Him is to rest in Him. As the psalmist declared: "The LORD is gracious and righteous; our God is full of compassion. The LORD protects the simplehearted; when I was in

great need, he saved me. Be at rest once more, O my soul,
for the LORD has been good to you" (Ps. 116:5–7).[13]

Albert Einstein helped to develop the laws of classic physics
with his theory of relativity, presented in 1905, and his theory
of general relativity, developed in the years of 1911–1915, that
explain movement and gravitational pulls of the planets and their
influence on all of life. These laws of physics rest on the certainty
of measured values, like a clockwork machine. In fact, classical
physics insists on measurable quantities and consistency.

However, for the study of the *subatomic* world of microscopic
atoms and particles, like protons and neutrons, the reality of
classic physics as we know it must be redefined. Between 1900
and 1930, Albert Einstein, Max Plank, Paul Dirac, Wolfgang
Pauli, and others formulated the theory of *quantum mechanics*, which tries to provide accurate and precise descriptions for
many phenomena that the "classical" theories of physics simply
cannot explain.[14] However, the "laws" of quantum mechanics
had to be defined by terms like *indeterminism, chance, unpredictability, randomness*, and *uncertainty*—words that were heresy to
the ordered laws of classic physics.

At first, Albert Einstein hated the fact that, on the subatomic
level, unpredictability, randomness, and uncertainty seemed
the rule rather than the exception. While classic physics insists
on precision, the universe proves to be indeterministic at its
most basic level. When you try to measure the existence of
microscopic particles that form the building blocks of life, you
encounter uncertainty. It seems more like a cosmic game of dice
than orderly precision. Einstein was appalled. He insisted, "God
does not play dice with the universe." To the consternation of
Einstein, an atom, under scrutiny, could simply disappear.

Arthur Eddington (1882–1944), one of the most prominent
and important astrophysicists of his time, was one of the first
physicists who understood the early ideas of relativity along
with Albert Einstein. He concluded that the physicist draws up

an elaborate plan of the atom and then proceeds critically to erase each detail in turn. What is left is the atom of modern physics.[15] Physicist Paul Davies, an internationally acclaimed physicist, writer, and broadcaster, is Professor of Natural Philosophy in the Australian Centre for Astrobiology, Macquarie University, Sydney.[16] He describes atoms and subatomic particles as inhabiting a shadowy world of half-existence.

An atom in subatomic space is like cotton candy that dissolves in our mouths—it disappears when we put it under scrutiny. You can't say anything about the future of these tiny particles that live a shadowy, ghostly, otherworldly existence. The unseen world on the molecular level simply does not follow prescribed rules or laws. Part of the problem is that the dimensions at the atomic level are occupied by seemingly empty space. The distance between atoms is a thousand times greater than the size of the atom. Even the atom itself is empty space. And 99.9 percent of the mass of a tiny atom is contained in its nucleus. Yet, the nucleus only occupies one hundred thousand billionth of the space of the entire atom. In this microscopic, sub-atomic world, matter possesses a degree of fuzziness, which cannot be precisely calculated or measured. [17]

And dimensions are not the only difference between the subatomic space and the world as we know it. The *behavior* of subatomic particles also differs greatly from the larger world. Every quantum bit has the potentiality to be here and there, now and then, a multiple capacity to act on the world, doing several different things at the same time. So startling were these discoveries, that Albert Einstein considered them heretical to the laws of physics. His friend, Neils Bohr wrote to him and told him to stop telling God what to do with His universe. Only after years of observing the mysteries of the microscopic world, which is much like going into a blind alley where no one has come out with satisfactory explanations, was Einstein finally able to accept its bizarre behavior.[18]

When this subatomic world was first explored in the early

part of the twentieth century, it was also theologically threatening to some. Where was the precision of God as seen in the rest of the universe? Max Planck, one of the original scientists to formulate the theory of quantum mechanics in 1902, was not spiritually shaken about its implications. He said, "Both science and religion wage a tireless battle against skepticism and dogmatism, against unbelief and superstition, with the goal: toward God."[19]

Dr. Swenson concludes that quantum mechanics occupies the interface where physics and metaphysics meet. And he says he is glad that God doesn't reveal all of His secrets to us. We might ask how does it all work in such harmony on a macro level, yet when you examine it on a subatomic level it is so indefinable and mysterious? Obviously God wants us to see the beauty, power, and precision on a larger scale. But when we look at the subatomic reality, which is mysterious and indefinable, it points to God's sovereignty and His desire to reserve glory for Himself.[20]

We worry when we try to anticipate God, not having an infinitesimal grasp of how great God's power is and how thorough, precise, and faithful He is. Science confirms the reality of God's brilliance. Yet, He can never be pinned down, as quantum physics shows us. He is life. He inhabits dimensions more profound than we can imagine. And He is love. His great love for us is measured by Calvary—the death of Christ, God's Son, to redeem mankind to eternal relationship with Himself.

Considering scientific realities can be a catalyst to recognizing our own frailty and finiteness when we consider the infinite power of God. As a result, we will be humbled and will listen more carefully when He speaks. When He says, "Be still, and know that I am God" (Ps. 46:10), we will understand that He cares about us more than a billion galaxies. He works in our lives in a thousand ways at once. And the more we trust His sovereign rule, the less we worry about our future. There is no more comforting doctrine.[21]

Dr. Swenson concludes that the problem of perspective lies with us:

> The problem is the dimness on our side. God is undefeated and He is for us. In the end, sovereignty wins and His glory will be unrestrained. Finally, God will deliver us from our dimness, and we will rest under the shelter of the Most High.[22]

The apostle Paul encouraged the church at Ephesus "to grasp how wide and long and high and deep is the love of Christ, and to know this love that surpasses knowledge—that you may be filled to the measure of all the fullness of God" (Eph. 3:18–19). He described God's power working in our lives in this striking way:

> Now to him who is able to do immeasurably more than all we ask or imagine, according to his power that is at work within us, to him be glory in the church and in Christ Jesus throughout all generations, for ever and ever! Amen.
>
> —EPHESIANS 3:20–21

Understanding the reality of God in the unfathomable wonders of the cosmos can help your faith and challenge you to forsake your worry habits and anxious thoughts and to grasp the greatness of His love for you. In meditating on the grandeur of God's reality in the cosmos, you can learn to rest in His sovereign power and redemptive love for you. As you pursue relationship with Christ, you can lay aside anxious thoughts and fill your mind and heart with God's infinite love and power. Then you will find ultimate satisfaction in fulfilling His purpose for your life.

Discussion Questions

1. Have you considered the reality of God in the cosmos? What scientific fact discussed here impacted your sense of God's omnipotence? How did it impress you?

_____

_____

_____

_____

2. How does the brief discussion of quantum physics impact your thinking? Is its lack of precision a problem to you? How does God's omnipotence relate to the unpredictability of these microscopic building blocks of life?

_____

_____

_____

_____

3. Consider the power of God demonstrated in these miracles of Jesus: Turning water into wine (John 2:9); walking on water (Matthew 14:25); appearing to the disciples, the doors being shut (John 20:19). How do they demonstrate the omnipotence of God, His love, and His sovereign rule over creation?

_____

_____

_____

_____

_____

For further reflection

Read Genesis chapters 1–3 and meditate on the reality of God in the creation of the cosmos.

Chapter 5

A NEW PERSPECTIVE

W ORRY COMES FROM the Old English term *wyrgan*, which means "to choke or strangle."[1] Worry can creep into our lives and strangle us. Jesus says in Mark 4:19, "The worries of this life, the deceitfulness of wealth and the desires for other things come in and choke the word, making it unfruitful."

Each of us is tempted by the desires of the world. For some, it's clothes or cars. For others, it's a relationship or a career. All of us battle selfish desires to see, measure, and own the tangible possessions of the world.

Do you worry about keeping your possessions, health, status, or position in life? Jesus tells us to change our focus.

> Do not store up for yourselves treasures on earth, where moth and rust destroy, and where thieves break in and steal. But store up for yourselves treasures in heaven, where moth and rust do not destroy, and where thieves do not break in and steal. For where your treasure is, there your heart will be also.
>
> —MATTHEW 6:19–21

Jesus tells us not to concern ourselves too much with earthly goods. We should be more concerned, He says, about eternal treasures. When we look at this world through eyes focused on the eternal God, we see His blessings. We appreciate Him for who He is and we are humbly grateful for the gift of life He has given us. Our hearts are filled with His love and we desire to return that love in worship and adoration to Him. We don't care whether we have more material possessions. We do care about loving and serving God with thanksgiving every day, and about letting that love guide our actions and attitudes in our relationships with others. Being aligned with God helps us care for others—a sure antidote to selfishness.

It's natural to be concerned about having adequate food, shelter, and clothes. But when worldly values creep into our thinking, we've chosen earthly treasures over the heavenly. We've chosen to turn our backs on God's Word, creating a void in our lives. The world tells us the way to fill the void is by getting more from our profession, relationships, appearance, status in life, money, and possessions.

So we worry about keeping what we have and about getting more. We worry about whether we can trust others, because we think everybody is just looking out for themselves. We worry about making the right impression on the right people so they'll think we are important. We find ourselves feeling we need to own places, people, and possessions; then we worry about whether we can keep them. We thought we would be free when we had enough money, friends, power, and influence. We thought we could "have it all," and now all of it has us. We're spinning around struggling to maintain our lifestyle.

Now, where are our treasures?

God wants to give us a new vision of life. Think of it as our Father owning the land on both sides of the river. One side is the present; the other side is eternity. We will be eternally cared for by Him. There is nothing we could want that He can't provide. Freedom from want frees us from worry. We have no fears of loss or even death. He has promised to let us live in His presence forever. We have the freedom of that eternal bliss of being engulfed with Him.

> So we fix our eyes not on what is seen, but on what is unseen. For what is seen is temporary, but what is unseen is eternal.
>
> —2 CORINTHIANS 4:18

Earthly treasures are fleeting. Living in the presence of God lasts for eternity. Thanks be to God for the eternity we have with Him! It is this eternal perspective and hope that fills our hearts with adoration for our Creator-Redeemer. Adoration is the spontaneous heart response to a revelation of our eternal God, who desires intimate relationship with His children. Adoration for our God fills us with praise and thanksgiving for His gift of life. It is in this posture of worship that we conquer fear and worry. And adoration brings us to repentance for our great sin of omission—a lack of appreciation that takes all of life for granted.

Let me share with you a story about a man who was engulfed by the eternal presence of God. Martyn Lloyd-Jones, a former physician, served as minister of London's Westminster Chapel for thirty years and was widely regarded as a powerful British preacher. As he grew older and weaker, near his death in 1981, his doctor said to him, "I don't like to see you so weary and worn and sad like this." "No," he said. "Not sad."[2] And he wasn't. He knew he had nothing to fear. He knew he had the kingdom of God. He would spend eternity with his Creator, Redeemer, and Sustainer.

> Do not be afraid, little flock, for your Father has been pleased to give you the kingdom.
>
> — LUKE 12:32

The kingdom of God is characterized by "righteousness, peace and joy" (Romans 14:17). And when we go beyond this life into eternity, the bliss that awaits us is indescribable. When the apostle John caught a glimpse of God's eternal kingdom, he described it this way:

> Now I saw…the holy city, New Jerusalem, coming down out of heaven from God, prepared as a bride adorned for her husband. And I heard a loud voice from heaven saying, "Behold, the tabernacle of God is with men, and He

will dwell with them, and they shall be His people. God Himself will be with them and be their God. And God will wipe away every tear from their eyes; there shall be no more death, nor sorrow, nor crying. There shall be no more pain, for the former things have passed away.

—Revelation 21:1–4, nkjv

Our Father has given us His eternal kingdom. In light of that wonderful spiritual reality, the importance of everything else pales in comparison. Of no importance are the jobs we have or the possessions we own. Of great importance are the eternal matters—such as our home with God in heaven. Our earthly possessions are His blessings, and we should praise Him for giving us such gifts. But our true home, our true security, is found in relationship with the Person of Jesus Christ. Being a member of His kingdom gives us a place, beginning now and lasting through eternity.

To cultivate this kind of eternal perspective, we need to adjust our temporal priorities, earning enough to meet the needs of our daily lives without allowing those needs to consume our thoughts and energies. As we place our focus on our eternal future with God, we become consumed with a future that begins now, enjoying His eternal presence in our daily lives. We bow our hearts in worship and adoration for His love, His faithfulness, and His sovereign care in our lives. In that way, we live in anticipation of heaven, spending eternity in His presence. And we make our life decisions based on that perspective.

Martin Luther said, "I live as though Jesus died yesterday, He rose today and is coming back again tomorrow."[3]

Think of Jesus as dying only yesterday. Calvary was yesterday. The power of the resurrection was yesterday. The power we live by today is the Holy Spirit. We live with Jesus today. Tomorrow, we look forward to His grace for eternity.

Therefore, I tell you, do not worry about your life, what you will eat or drink; or about your body, what you will wear. Is not life more important than food, and the body more important than clothes? Look at the birds of the air; they do not sow or reap or store away in barns, and yet your heavenly Father feeds them. Are you not much more valuable than they? Who of you by worrying can add a single hour to his life?

And why do you worry about clothes? See how the lilies of the field grow. They do not labor or spin. Yet I tell you that not even Solomon in all his splendor was dressed like one of these. If that is how God clothes the grass of the field, which is here today and tomorrow is thrown into the fire, will he not much more clothe you, O you of little faith? So do not worry, saying, "What shall we eat?" or "What shall we drink?" or "What shall we wear?" For the pagans run after all these things, and your heavenly Father knows that you need them. But seek first his kingdom and his righteousness, and all these things will be given to you as well.

—MATTHEW 6:25–33

In these verses, Jesus is explicit in His instruction not to worry. He puts our concerns in proper perspective. We are of much greater value than the birds and flowers that God takes care of. We have nothing to fear because the Lord knows what we need and He will give it to us, now and for eternity. This reality should humble us and fill our hearts with deep appreciation for the loving care of our heavenly Father. As we express our thanksgiving and gratitude for His love, our hearts are filled with His peace.

Jesus wants us to be free from the worries and anxieties that can rule our daily lives. He wants us to see our lives from God's point of view, not man's. He wants us to see the world around us as short-lived, our problems as temporary. He wants us to take our focus off our own needs and desires and plans; that's thinking by the standards of this world. Instead, He wants us to focus on eternity in His presence. God will take care of our problems; all we need to do is rest in His presence. When we understand that, how can we worry about the events and circumstances of this world? We have all of eternity with Christ stretching out before us.

Dietrich Bonhoeffer, as he faced execution by the Germans during World War II, said, "This is the end, but also the beginning."[4] Each of us can live with the anticipation of heaven in our hearts. His presence is relevant to our daily lives—our jobs, our relationships, our mental thoughts and attitudes, our rising in the morning and resting at night, and our continual thanksgiving for that eternity.

This eternal perspective has practical applications. Here are five steps each of us can take to diagnose and analyze our worries.

1. **Take one day at a time.** "This is the day the LORD has made; let us rejoice and be glad in it" (Ps. 118:24). We are often so busy smothering the present moment with worries about tomorrow or regrets about yesterday that we kill today. Don't worry about tomorrow or six months from now. Don't worry if the government is going to take over the medical system or if social security is going to go broke. We just need to do the very best we can where we are with what we have. Don't worry about the rest. Tomorrow belongs to God. We have no control over the future, but He has promised to provide for us eternally. We have only today; let us enjoy it and be thankful.

2. **Get the facts.** Write down all the information you have for the situation you're worried about. Keep a list on paper, not in your head. Not everything comes quickly, but write down all the details and

analyze them. "What exactly is it that I'm worried about? What are the consequences? How does it really affect me?" As we write down our worries, we become followers who trust in God to provide and who see Him at work.

3. **Analyze the results.** As we think through a worrisome situation, we often realize it's not the event that troubles us—it's the anticipation of the event. We realize certain things are going to happen regardless of what we do. Those that can't be cured must be endured. And we can endure them because we know God is in control now and for eternity. Our attitude of thanksgiving will help us put Him first and trust in His goodness and kindness to us.

4. **Improve upon the worst.** Business people always look at a problem by projecting the worst possible scenario. Then they put their energy into ensuring that the worst won't happen. We can often improve the end result if we take positive steps to prevent the most negative results.

5. **Be done with it.** Put the worry behind you; you've done all you can to take care of the problem. Refuse to allow it to continue bothering you. Give the problem to God, with thanksgiving, and know that He can handle any situation. He is the King of kings and Lord of lords! When the cares try to reassert themselves, cast them on the Father afresh. Believe again in His sovereignty; apply His faithfulness to the details of life that seem to lure you into worry. Call your Jehovah Jireh—"The Lord will provide."

In paintings, artists use perspective to portray different views of the same object. As Christians, there is only one perspective we must have—the perspective of eternity. That perspective sets the tone for our lives. All our daily actions can be carried out against the background of eternity. Every decision, every action, every thought, every attitude is based on our eternal life through Christ. We're engulfed by Him and our lives are entwined with Him forever. Meditating on this spiritual reality will help us to more deeply appreciate our Savior and Lord. As we humbly bow before Him in expressing our love and adoration for His sovereign care for our souls, we will be overwhelmed with His love and peace. In His strength we can face all of life's challenges without fear or worry.

Discussion Questions

1. What material goods do you value? Do you think of them as earthly treasures? Why or why not?

_____

_____

_____

_____

2. What are treasures in heaven? Do you think of yourself as having them? List ways this affects your daily life.

_____

_____

_____

_____

3. Each of us has a weakness for some material possession or circumstance. What's yours? How does Satan use it to make you worry?

_____

_____

_____

_____

_____

4. Apply the five steps of analyzing worry to one current concern in your life. How does it help?

_____

_____

_____

_____

For further reflection

> For to me, to live is Christ and to die is gain.
> —PHILIPPIANS 1:21

Paul writes that everything he does on earth is to glorify the Person of Jesus Christ. And when he dies, he will be with Christ for eternity. So it makes no difference. If Christ is in everything we do, we don't have to worry about anything. All we have to do is rejoice and be thankful. Amen.

Chapter 6

WHO'S in CHARGE?

I N THE SPRING of 1980, a series of earthquakes and small eruptions drew the attention of people living in the Pacific Northwest. Scientists and sightseers were drawn to Mount St. Helens. Steam vents, tremors, and hot spots appeared almost daily. Then on May 18, a 5.1-magnitude earthquake shook the mountain. For a few seconds the north flank seemed to ripple, then broke loose and began sliding downhill as a massive avalanche. Eruption plumes shot up as quickly as 600 miles an hour. The blast traveled as a hot, churning mass of gas, rock, ash, and ice. More than fifty people were killed or reported missing after the blast, and the eruption devastated 235 square miles.[1]

The eruption of Mount St. Helens was a tragedy. It's also a powerful reminder that there are forces in this world over which we have no control. Even when the best scientific minds and equipment were keeping watch over the mountain, they could not predict what was going to happen next. It's the same way in our lives. More recently, tsunamis, hurricanes, wars, famines, and other large-scale tragedies have struck millions of people in our world, making them feel helpless in the face of devastating loss. Despite our best efforts and knowledge and abilities, there are some events and circumstances over which we have no control.

We can't control the stock market, which dictates how well our money might perform. We can't control another person's thoughts and feelings, which dictate how strong our relationships might be. And even if we eat right and exercise regularly, we can't completely control our health. Accidents, disease, and illness still happen.

Historian Barbara Tuchman said, "War is the unfolding of

miscalculations."[2] Much of what goes on between nations is based upon a struggle for control. When a nation believes it can control another, or when a government thinks it can control its citizens, it miscalculates and wars ensue.

On a personal level, miscalculations can be just as chaotic or devastating. When we act as though we understand and can control events, circumstances, and people, we make a huge mistake. Control is another form of selfishness. Trying to control situations or people shows that we've replaced our trust in God with faith in ourselves. But that kind of misplaced faith always results in failure.

Have you ever spent time with 2-year-olds? Some of their favorite phrases are "mine," "no," and "I do it." They want to be independent. They think they know what they're doing. They have faith in their developing skills and abilities and judgment. Sometimes that streak of independence is frustrating to parents who have to wait as the child struggles to climb in and out of a car seat by himself. Sometimes it is dangerous. No matter how smart or capable a 2-year-old is, he should not play with the stove or try to cross the street by himself.

But children persist in testing the limits of their independence. For instance, there's the little one who uses the kitchen drawers like a ladder to climb up to the counter. Like a kitten caught up in a tree, he gets stuck in a situation he's not equipped to handle. And only then does he start to worry about how he'll get down. Then comes the cry for help.

How often are we like that with God? Have you ever wanted to do it yourself rather than wait for Him? What happened? I think all of us are tempted to rely on our own brains and brawn. When we put our faith in ourselves, we lose sight of God's love and care. We're like that 2-year-old climbing onto the kitchen counter. Once we get stuck, we get scared.

> In my distress I called to the LORD; I cried to my God for
> help. From his temple he heard my voice; my cry came

before him, into his ears…He brought me out into a spacious place; he rescued me because he delighted in me.

—PSALM 18:6, 19

In order to know the personal presence of God in our lives, we must recognize the sovereign power of God as our Creator–Redeemer. To find our purpose in His kingdom, we must give Him His rightful place as absolute sovereign deity. God's *sovereignty* speaks of His ruling over all as an all-wise King—benevolent, gracious, majestic, and powerful: "Our God is in heaven; he does whatever pleases him" (Ps. 115:3). God is love (1 John. 4:8). So we know it "pleases" Him to do good to His creation:

For the LORD Most High is awesome; He is a great King over all the earth. He will subdue the peoples under us, And the nations under our feet. He will choose our inheritance for us…Sing praises to our King, sing praises! For God is the King of all the earth.

—PSALM 47:2–4, 6–7, NKJV

God declared His sovereignty through the prophet, Isaiah:

Remember the former things of old, For I am God, and there is no other; I am God, and there is none like Me, Declaring the end from the beginning, And from ancient times things that are not yet done, Saying, "My counsel shall stand, And I will do all My pleasure.

—ISAIAH 46:9–10, NKJV

God reveals His sovereignty through His providential guidance and care. The Scriptures reveal His guiding hand throughout the history of mankind. And modern history corroborates the kindness of His providence. During wartime, soldiers have experienced inexplicable rescues and supernatural aid. Testimonies of divine intervention in the lives of children, miraculous cures, and protection from natural disasters all testify to the goodness of God's providential care.

Rx for Worry

When we integrate the reality of God's sovereignty into our faith, His grace is manifest in our lives. We focus on His grace—His divine favor to us as created beings—and we seek His provision for our salvation through His Son, Jesus Christ. Then we begin to appreciate God as our Father, Redeemer, Provider, and Friend. When we begin to understand that all things exist because of the sovereign power of God, our only response is to bow in adoration and worship before Him.

What a consolation to know that a power greater than ourselves can restore us! God wants to keep us safe. He doesn't do it out of a sense of obligation. He does it because He loves us. As a faithful shepherd watches diligently over his sheep, the Lord, our Shepherd, delights in caring for us. Not only that, He's told us that He will eternally provide—in this world and the next. He wants us to trust Him to provide.

When we're selfish, we care deeply about how much we have. We try to control what we have and we calculate ways to get more. But if we're trusting in God, we don't care whether we have more or less. We know He will provide for us regardless.

> Trust in the LORD with all your heart, And lean not on your own understanding; In all your ways acknowledge Him, And He shall direct your paths.
> —PROVERBS 3:5–6, NKJV

We have to trust in God and let Him guide us. We have to hand Him our independence and our desire for control. We have to let Him take the reins of our lives in His hands.

Trust is not always easy. We've grown to like the beliefs and values of the world, even if we're filled with worry. We're in the habit of trusting ourselves, not trusting God. We're comfortable with the lifestyle of work and worry that we've developed.

We must let go of worldly attitudes so we can firmly grasp God's hand. We must acknowledge His great faithfulness to us as well as His divine sovereignty in our lives. Then we can let

Him lead us. We can give Him control of our lives, and we can walk in trust and thanksgiving.

> When I am afraid, I will trust in you. In God, whose word
> I praise, in God I trust; I will not be afraid. What can
> mortal man do to me?
>
> —PSALM 56:3–4

I memorized this passage years ago. It helps me align myself with God and His Word. It reminds me that God is in control and that I don't need to be afraid or try to be in charge myself. Reciting these verses in times of trouble has helped me worry less and trust more. God's Word can help you, too.

Discussion Questions

1. What circumstances beyond your control do you worry about? How can you release your desire for control?

   _____

   _____

   _____

   _____

2. When are you selfish? When are you reluctant to trust in God's ability to provide?

   _____

   _____

   _____

   _____

   _____

3. List some reasons why you can trust God.

_____

_____

_____

_____

4. Memorize Psalm 56:3–4 this week. Then recite
   these verses the next time you need encouragement
   about God's provision. List here how the verses
   helped.

_____

_____

_____

_____

For further reflection

> The LORD is near to all who call on him, to all who call on
> him in truth. He fulfills the desires of those who fear him;
> he hears their cry and saves them.
>
> —PSALM 145:18–19

God is in control of our lives and eternity. We can call on
Him and He will save us. Share some examples of how He has
done this in your life.

Chapter 7

PEACE in GOD'S PROMISES

"I'm getting gray-haired from worrying."

"Why are you worried?"

"Because I'm getting gray hair."

T HIS FICTITIOUS CONVERSATION might sound trite, but it shows the destructive cycle worry creates. Once we start to worry about one area of our lives, it becomes easier to worry about another, and soon all we do is worry. Some patients I see are always worrying. I can offer many reassurances and give them all the information they need, yet they still worry. They're in the habit of worrying—about their cataract surgery, about their cars, about everything you could imagine. These folks' first reaction to a problem is worry.

Any of us could let worry become a way of thinking and a way of life. Worry produces more negative thoughts. And negative thoughts produce negative people. I've been around negative people in my life, and I don't like it. I'm sure you've been around them, too. Negative people constantly complain and criticize. Nothing is ever good enough for them.

When worry sets in, we need to condition ourselves to respond in faith, not fear. The best way to replace that bad habit of worry is with a good one—looking to God's promises rather than our own feeble, human solutions. These promises are His own words. He reminds us that He will intervene. He will help us. He will give fresh courage and strength. He will calm the storms in our lives.

> Taste and see that the LORD is good; blessed is the man
> who takes refuge in him. Fear the LORD, you his saints,

57

for those who fear him lack nothing. The lions may grow
weak and hungry, but those who seek the LORD lack no
good thing.

—PSALM 34:8–10

Throughout the Bible, God promises to provide for us. We
should have no doubts, no fears, and no worries. We must
remember God's pledges and promises to provide, especially in
those times when we're tempted to worry rather than to trust
in His faithfulness.

The Blame Game

Chronic worriers tend to quit taking responsibility for their
actions. As children, they say, "My mother won't let me do this
or that," or, "The school won't let me do this." As they mature,
they continue to find external reasons for their problems. They
believe they have no control over the events in their lives, but
that other people do. They act like they are pawns or victims.

They look to others for reasons for their own problems, but
they don't look to God as the solution for their problems. First
they need to see that God loves them and will provide for them.
They need to surrender their lives to God, having faith in His
eternal promises and grace. Nothing can conquer those who
truly believe in Him.

We are hard pressed on every side, but not crushed; perplexed, but not in despair; persecuted, but not abandoned;
struck down, but not destroyed. We always carry around
in our body the death of Jesus, so that the life of Jesus may
also be revealed in our body.

—2 CORINTHIANS 4:8–10

They must take these promises and believe that they have the
freedom to make positive choices, which will benefit them to
the glory of God. God has given them the ability to take respon-

sibility for their actions and their lives.

Blame looks to the past, which can't be changed; but responsibility looks to the future, which can be taken care of and managed through the grace of God.

Do We Measure Up?

There are times in each of our lives when we compare ourselves with others. We might get jealous of the new car our neighbor buys, or if someone else in the company gets the promotion we should have had. We might even wonder whether our children are as successful as the children of our friends.

Jesus talks about this attitude in the parable of the Prodigal Son. Most of the story is about the younger son, who took his inheritance and wasted it all. When the younger son came home, his father welcomed him with open arms and threw a huge party. When the older son heard about the party, he was furious. He thought it was unfair that his father should be so generous with someone the son judged as undeserving.

> Look! All these years I've been slaving for you and never disobeyed your orders. Yet you never gave me even a young goat so I could celebrate with my friends. But when this son of yours who has squandered your property with prostitutes comes home, you kill the fattened calf for him!
>
> LUKE 15:29–30

The older brother wanted his father to be fair. But his father, like any father, was more than fair. He was loving. This was his response:

> My son...you are always with me, and everything I have is yours. But we had to celebrate and be glad, because this brother of yours was dead and is alive again; he was lost and is found.
>
> —LUKE 15:31–32

59

R̶ for Worry

The father had a greater vision. He loved both of his sons, and that was more than enough. God is the same way with us. As much as we might worry or complain about another's success, we need to remember that God loves each of us. And His love for one person doesn't have anything to do with His love for someone else. All we should do is look to Him.

> Do not fret because of evil men or be envious of those who do wrong; for like the grass they will soon wither, like green plants they will soon die away. Trust in the LORD and do good; dwell in the land and enjoy safe pasture. Delight yourself in the LORD and he will give you the desires of your heart. Commit your way to the LORD; trust in him and he will do this: He will make your righteousness shine like the dawn, the justice of your cause like the noonday sun. Be still before the LORD and wait patiently for him; do not fret when men succeed in their ways, when they carry out their wicked schemes. Refrain from anger and turn from wrath; do not fret—it leads only to evil. For evil men will be cut off, but those who hope in the LORD will inherit the land.
>
> —PSALM 37:1–9

But it's not just comparing our lives with others that cause us to worry. We also worry about whether other people like us and accept us.

As I grew up, I saw young girls whose parents didn't accept them. They worked out their sexuality in a way that cost them satisfaction in their lives, and they ruined everything by not allowing the Lord to work. They never had peace. They ended up trying to find acceptance in every circumstance and person and place, but not in the Lord.

If we dare to take our eyes off people and turn them to God, we can be freed from the destructive forces that grip our lives. God calls all of us to receive His grace. It is the goodness of God that makes Him desire to bestow His favor upon us. The goodness of God is unfathomable. There is nothing as great as His eternal love; nothing that can satisfy our hearts like His abiding presence in our lives. He desires that His children experience this total well-being of body, mind, and spirit.

Not only does the grace of God bring salvation to our hearts (Eph. 2:8), it also keeps us in the love of God, protecting us from destructive forces in our lives. His love satisfies our hearts and gives us purpose in life. The apostle Paul learned to say: "By the grace of God I am what I am" (1 Cor. 15:10). It is not what people think or say about us that should affect our lives fundamentally. It is what God says about us that we should value and believe.

The desire for acceptance is strong in human nature. If we don't embrace the grace of God's acceptance of us in Christ, we can act out in many ways to seek acceptance from others. We may be reckless in the way we drive a car or run a business or spend money. We may become belligerent, aggressive, or violent, trying to earn others' acceptance and respect. And we may be sexually irresponsible, seeking a false sense of security and love.

Even as believers, if we're busy worrying about what others think of us, we become selfish; we would not be aligned with God. Our relationship with the Lord would decline. It's like a relationship with a person with whom we were close but now we're distant. We can't really talk to them; there's no closeness anymore. The telephone wires to the Lord seem to be cut down. We do that simply, and I mean very simply, by being critical or envious of others and being worried about how we compare with them.

We're worried about the attitudes of others toward us, rather than our attitude toward God. We need to get back in the good habit of practicing faith and remembering His grace. If God accepts us as believing sinners through the cross of Christ, and if He will provide everything we need, why should we be worried about what others think and do?

We should be filling our minds with our relationship with

God and spending our time in His presence. We need to realize there is nothing as important as God and our relationship with Him. This eternal perspective helps us be more free and joyful, less anxious and worried, and less critical and judgmental.

Fear of Loneliness

Alone, alone, all, all alone,
Alone on a wide wide sea!
And never a saint took pity on
My soul in agony.
—THE RIME OF THE ANCIENT MARINER
SAMUEL TAYLOR COLERIDGE

Each of us has an inner longing for the eternal God. When it's not filled with a connection with God, we become lonely. Our hearts are seeking something, and the many possessions and jobs and relationships we have tried don't seem to be it. We believe if we just rush around enough, keep busy enough, and surround ourselves with enough important and interesting people, our loneliness will disappear.

We often fear this loneliness, and we try to ignore it by manipulating others to get love and attention from them. Or we try to fill the void by seeking people as possessions, not as genuine relationships. "Loneliness and the feeling of being unwanted is the most terrible poverty," Mother Teresa said.[1] This fear is very dangerous. It causes many people to make bad choices regarding friends and marriage partners. The fear of not really being loved causes many people to enter into harmful relationships and wrong marriages.

But we are fulfilled emotionally only when we give ourselves to Christ in a personal, love relationship with Him. Loneliness is banished when we are truly connected with the Lord. The Bible doesn't simply say that God *loves* or that He *has* love; it states plainly: "God *is* love" (1 John 4:8, emphasis added). We were created by love. Is it any wonder that the human heart craves love so deeply, and on so many levels? We were made by love—to walk in relationship with God, who is love. Blaise Pascal, the seventeenth century French physicist and philosopher wrote:

> There is a God shaped vacuum in the heart of every man which cannot be filled by any created thing, but only by God, the Creator, made known through Jesus.[2]

Learning to appreciate God's presence in our lives by receiving Christ is imperative if we are to satisfy our deepest desire for love. Knowing the love of God personally helps us to make divine connections with others through the Holy Spirit.

Another cure for loneliness is friendship with godly friends. These friendships are selective, sacrificial, steadfast, and secure. Friendships are special when they are totally committed; when each person is willing to do anything for the other. Lives are no longer empty and lonely. Personal relationship with Christ changes who we are. And the presence of God is working in our friendships to make our lives more meaningful.

The Lure of Money

> People who want to get rich fall into temptation and a trap and into many foolish and harmful desires that plunge men into ruin and destruction. For the love of money is a root of all kinds of evil.
>
> —1 TIMOTHY 6:9–10

We frequently worry about money. We are in awe of it. It is the world's measuring stick of accomplishments. The world tells us that we will succeed and gain respect if we earn enough money. The world's life is determined by money—money status, money power, money obtained from work, money needed, the fear of not having enough money in the future, and the fear of losing the money presently in hand.

We can think about money more than we think about God. We can end up worshiping money and have no time to worship God. Money can displace God from our lives. It becomes our god. I've seen myself, and many other people, who are very interested in the Lord, do it. When we're focused on money, we think about it in such a way that we worry and are not at peace.

The deceitfulness of riches is that money promises everything; it appears to give some things, but in reality it gives nothing. In the end, money lets us down. When we worry that we won't have enough money to meet our needs, we do not trust the Lord to provide. We forget His eternal perspective. We allow our fears to control us. The fear of running out can be worse than actually running out.

That worry is more harmful to us than any decreased financial status. It ages us, it changes our judgment, it consumes and controls our lives; it takes us away from God. Our relationship to money puts us in bondage. How can we worship God on Sunday and cheat on our taxes—or anything else—throughout the week? The mind games we play show that we are devious and not devoted to God. We are being untrue. Money is not worth our cheating to get it. We fool ourselves if we think finances are of such great importance.

Our true worth is not measured by having money in the bank or cars and houses. Our true worth was measured on the cross and is reflected by our response in faith and thanksgiving to Jesus' death and resurrection. Our sustenance is the presence of Jesus in our lives. Jesus taught: "Watch out! Be on your guard against all kinds of greed; a man's life does not consist in the abundance of his possessions" (Luke 12:15).

Counting the Cost

Here's a favorite exercise of mine. If I start getting too worried or anxious about a situation, I like to take a step back from it. I may even walk up to a mirror, look myself in the face, and ask, "Is this worth the worry?" Jesus poses the same question:

> Are not five sparrows sold for two pennies? Yet not one of them is forgotten by God. Indeed, the very hairs of your head are all numbered. Don't be afraid; you are worth more than many sparrows.
>
> —LUKE 12:6–7

God loves us and treasures us as His children. He has everything under control for all eternity. All we need to do is remember to look to Him and let Him provide. Praise be to God for His infinite wisdom and mercy! Amen.

Discussion Questions

1. Do you know someone who plays "the blame game"? How can knowing 2 Corinthians 4:8–10 help?

_____

_____

_____

2. When have you compared yourself with others? How does it help you? How does it hurt you?

_____

_____

_____

_____

3. When have you felt lonely? What helps you out of that feeling?

_____

_____

_____

4. What helps you find meaningful relationships with others?

_____

_____

_____

5. How important is money to you? Do you think you have enough? What does God say about how much is enough?

_____

_____

_____

For further reflection

Set your minds on things above, not on earthly things.
—COLOSSIANS 3:2

The only way to mature in God is to put Him first. List five ways you can do this in your daily life.

Chapter 8

A PERSONAL STORY

T HROUGH THE YEARS I've met many people who have had to battle fear and worry. I'd like to share with you the story of one of my patients. Because of a previous condition with one eye before she came to St. Luke's Cataract and Laser Institute, she was very anxious. She struggled with fear before her eye surgery at St. Luke's, and we spent time discussing the habit of worry and fear she had built up over the years. After her eye surgery, she wrote me this letter detailing her struggles with fear and her victories over worry.

Fear and How I Am Overcoming It

Dear Dr. Gills,

I have been ruled by a four-letter word all my life—Fear.

I remember being in bed at night when I was 4 or 5 years old and being afraid. I would be afraid to turn my back to the wall, thinking a big witch would come out of the wall and "get me." I remember it very well to this day.

Then I remember being scared by a movie my parents took me to. They let me sleep with them for a few nights, but they got tired of that. They made me walk the living room floor to tire me out so I'd go into my own bedroom. I got tired, but was still scared (it was an awful movie), so I wouldn't give in. I remember crying and crying, and being so tired and feeling I just had to take this punishment and fear. In other words, I was a real victim.

Growing up, and as an adult, I was always afraid of something going wrong or happening to my body. Results of tests and so forth would worry me so. I was not scared of other hardships or disappointments in my life—just my body.

Fear would take me over; I was always imagining the worst. It was not a fear of pain, but a fear of being helpless.

Even the expression on my face would and does become tense and tight, and the body language I'm sure reflects the same. This robbed my energy and made me feel tired all the time.

I had tremendous fears about my eyes after my first retina problem, which was detached. (This was a condition I had before I came to St. Luke's.) I was always afraid of "losing my eyesight." And I just couldn't find a way to handle this.

When I finally knew I had to get my one good eye operated on, I put it off as long as I could, until I couldn't live with that fear any longer and bit the bullet and set the date at St. Luke's.

I was a nervous wreck weeks before, even though I knew I had the best eye doctor in the world. I had utmost confidence in him. It was my eye I was scared of. My daughter gave me advice on one of the two ways I helped myself be less afraid before the surgery. She said, "The day before, get out and work off all that tense energy in your body. Walk and/or swim until you are so tired." I didn't feel like doing that; I was so used to being all tensed up. But I did. And it helped immensely.

But the most important thing: Through prayer I was able to finally "let go," surrender myself to whatever was God's will. I was thinking positively, but knowing and really accepting God's will to be for my best, and it was entirely in His hands.

Of course I can report I came out with better sight than I dreamed of, and with a loving, effortless procedure.

You have to face your fear, not just escape into TV or whatever and take your mind off it. You have to face, accept, and let go. Then fears escape you.

Now I know how much imagination has to do with fear. It's probably the whole thing. Because if you're actually face to face with a fearsome thing, like a lion, you have to do one of two things: run or fight him, and it's over. The worry and fearful thinking whether something could or would happen is really only in our imagination. So why can't we make the choices and substitute that fear-imagination with positive and good results? We must learn tools of how to do just that when the other pops in. Learn and fine-tune them until we only expect the best. This is the task. That is what I really have to learn and use, and I'm sure there are many others who need to also learn these tools.

I'm grateful to share this with you.

Valerie Tourin

Discussion Questions

1. The writer of this letter could remember being afraid as a child. What scared you as a young child?

_____

_____

_____

2. What scares you now? Do those fears change your behavior?

_____

_____

_____

3. List the tools you can use to face your fears this week.

_____

_____

_____

4. Describe an experience in which you applied these tools and overcame fear.

_____

_____

_____

For further reflection

> The LORD himself goes before you and will be with you; he will never leave you nor forsake you. Do not be afraid; do not be discouraged.
>
> —DEUTERONOMY 31:8

God tells us to not be afraid because He is with us. How do you know God is with you today?

Chapter 9

THE WEAPONS AGAINST WORRY: FAITH, GRACE, and THANKSGIVING

W ORRY TAKES ROOT in our lives when our selfish interest keeps us from being aligned with God's eternal purposes. We do not have His perspective of life, for the present or for the future. When we're selfish, we worry about material, earthly concerns in our lives and in the lives of those around us. We fear events and circumstances beyond our control. And chronic worry will destroy us. When we're worried, we can't think straight, we can't sort out our emotions, we act irrationally, and we eventually can kill ourselves with the stress that worry causes.

We need to ask ourselves what worries us. What's putting a brake on our physical, emotional, and spiritual health? How long have we had it? Can we release that brake? Can we get rid of the worry? Can we get rid of the selfishness?

Praise God that He has given believers victory over all sin— including selfishness and worry—through the Person of Jesus Christ! Jesus understands our human nature. It is worse to worry about being hungry than actually being hungry. Worse is worrying about having enough money to buy the right clothes. Worse is worrying about being able to live the way we want to live. Jesus knows worry destroys the beautiful peace that comes from God living within us.

He knows there's only one way to break the bonds of worry, and that is through Him. The basic treatment for worry is a life of thanksgiving for God's grace and faith in His provision, all built on the cross of Jesus' sacrifice. When we truly open our hearts to our Redeemer, we bow before Him in humble adoration and worship for His loving care. We value His presence in our lives more than anything else. And we can walk up the gangplank of faith, full of thanksgiving, into the ship of God's grace. We trust in His divine favor to meet the need of every situation we face.

A deeper understanding of faith, grace, and thanksgiving, through Christ, can help us defeat worry.

Faith

There is a story about a fellow from the country, who, after years of avoiding flying, had the thrill of his first airplane trip. He reached his destination and returned safely. Upon his return, a friend asked what he thought about the trip. "Well, to tell you the truth," he said, "I never did put all my weight down on the airplane."

Have you ever done that? There have been times in my own life when I've been reluctant to put all my weight down on Christ. I was just not quite sure I wanted Him to help me through a tough time or predicament. Then the inevitable happened. The situation got far worse. I should have trusted in the Lord in the first place.

Trusting ourselves is the opposite of what God wants us to do. He asks us to place our trust and confidence in His sovereign power and perfect love. He promises He will take care of us; we don't need to worry.

> I lift up my eyes to the hills—where does my help come from? My help comes from the LORD, the Maker of heaven and earth. He will not let your foot slip—he who watches over you will not slumber; indeed, he who watches over Israel will neither slumber nor sleep. The LORD watches over you—the LORD is your shade at your right hand; the sun will not harm you by day, nor the moon by night.

The LORD will keep you from all harm—he will watch
over your life; the LORD will watch over your coming and
going both now and forevermore.

—PSALM 121

What beautiful promises! Day and night, He will watch over
us. As any father watches over a child, God watches over us. We
can rest our entire weight on Him; we can have faith in Him.
And then our minds will be at peace.

Faith functions in our lives in almost unconscious ways. For
example, there is not a person alive who does not have faith in
the law of gravity. Perhaps as a child, you tried to defy gravity
with inevitable, and sometimes painful, consequences. All of our
actions are subjected to an understanding of the power of the
gravitational force under which we function. For example, when
you go into an exclusive shop where fine china or other exquisite
glass creations are sold, you are very careful not to drop a vase
you are admiring. You know that the law of gravity is working
and that such an accident would result in breaking valuable mer-
chandise. You have explicit faith in the law of gravity.

Yet, the law of gravity points us ever upward to faith in our
God who made us. Isaac Newton wrote in a letter in 1692: "So
then Gravity may put the Planets into Motion, but without the
divine Power it could never put them into such a circulating
motion as they have about the sun; and therefore, for this, as
well as other Reasons, I am compelled to ascribe the Frame of
the System to an intelligent Agent...The Cause of Gravity is
what I do not pretend to know."[1]

Dr. Swenson writes that although Sir Isaac Newton clarified
the law of gravity several hundred years ago, it remains a mysterious force. If we drop a pencil, it falls to the floor. Why? At
the deepest level, we still don't know. Yet if God were to suspend
the law of gravity, we would need a steel cable six hundred miles
in diameter to hold the moon in place.[2] As we pause to consider the mystery of the law of gravity, the wonder of creation

73

will transcend our finiteness and help us to place our faith in a sovereign, infinite God. Though God remains mysterious to our finite minds, as we place our faith in Him, we can acknowledge His power and surrender to His love.

There's one biblical account of total faith that always speaks to me. It's the story of a father who was willing to sacrifice what he loved most because he trusted in God.

In Genesis chapter 22, God tells Abraham to take Isaac, his only son, to the land of Moriah and sacrifice him as a burnt offering. Now, this seems like something Abraham wouldn't want to do. He and Sarah had waited so long to have Isaac. Would he want to give him up? What would he tell Sarah? And this act seems contrary to the promise God had made that "it is through Isaac that your offspring will be reckoned" (Gen. 21:12). But Abraham collected the wood for the burnt offering, packed up his donkey, and headed off with Isaac.

When they got close to Mount Moriah, Isaac got curious. He wanted to know where the lamb was for the burnt offering. "God himself will provide the lamb," (Gen. 22:8) Abraham said, showing total trust. They got to the place God directed, and Abraham started preparing for the sacrifice. He built the altar and arranged the wood. Then he tied up Isaac and put him on top of the wood. Finally, he pulled out his knife to kill his son. At that moment, the angel of the Lord called out to him:

> "Do not lay a hand on the boy," he said. "Do not do anything to him. Now I know that you fear God, because you have not withheld from me your son, your only son."
>
> —Genesis 22:12

And then Abraham saw a ram caught in some bushes, and he took it and sacrificed it in place of his son. "To this day it is said, 'On the mountain of the LORD it will be provided'" (Gen. 22:14). A new name was given to this spot, to encourage all believers to cheerfully trust in God: Jehovah Jireh, "the Lord will provide."

Abraham's encounter helps me remember that God, as our Father and as our Shepherd, will always provide. Faith is a great weapon against worry. I know He will provide. And I know this not just in my head, but in my heart. I know He's intimately involved in my daily life.

> I have been crucified with Christ and I no longer live, but Christ lives in me. The life I live in the body, I live by faith in the Son of God, who loved me and gave himself for me.
> —GALATIANS 2:20

Living fully in the kingdom of God is a life of faith. We need to focus on God in all the moments of our days, noticing His work in our lives and appreciating and thanking Him. Prayerfully, we do our planning, lay the groundwork, act responsibly, and trust God for the results. The Scripture is full of wonderful promises for the intervention of God in the details of our life's situations: "Trust in the LORD with all your heart and lean not on your own understanding; in all your ways acknowledge him, and he will make your paths straight" (Prov. 3:5–6).

The Scriptures also teach that faith is a gift of God to us. We cannot manufacture it. The faith that brings us to salvation through Christ is a gift of God (Eph. 2:8–9). After receiving the gift of salvation, we must seek to grow in our faith through reading of the Scriptures, prayer, and exercising our faith to uproot the unbelief in our minds. This unbelief often manifests itself as thoughts of fear and worry and lack of trust in our Lord's faithfulness and sovereignty.

As we read the Scriptures, we learn to appreciate God's love and faithfulness toward us and we begin to be filled with faith in Him. That faith is expressed through praise and thanksgiving, worship and adoration. Pursuing growth in faith is vitally important if we want to please God:

> And without faith it is impossible to please God, because anyone who comes to him must believe that he exists and

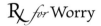

that he rewards those who earnestly seek him.

—HEBREWS 11:6

Faith is the essence of our strength in the eternal God. Then joy, peace, and hope can blossom forth because we know we will be provided for. We can be totally content in Him, because we know we have everything we need through the Person of Jesus Christ. George Mueller once said it this way: "Where faith begins, anxiety ends; for where anxiety begins, faith ends."[3]

Life hits us in waves of good events and bad circumstances. These can create anxiety and joy, happiness and fear. Satan would love to use those bad times to undermine our faith. He would love for us to give in to our fears and anxieties. He would love for us to forget God's promises of provision and start to rely on our weak human efforts. He would love for us to worry.

But faith says we're content in our present state. Faith says we have enough, whether we are rich or poor, healthy or sick, young or old. Regardless of circumstances and events, we know our daily strength comes from the Lord. The only real security and stability we have is in Jesus Christ. We must stand firm in faith, knowing God provides.

Paul, who was imprisoned many times, shows us we can be happy and content regardless of our circumstances because we have faith in Christ. Locked in prison, Paul still rejoiced because his joy was in Christ, not in external circumstances.

> I am not saying this because I am in need, for I have learned
> to be content whatever the circumstances. I know what it
> is to be in need, and I know what it is to have plenty. I
> have learned the secret of being content in any and every
> situation, whether well fed or hungry, whether living in
> plenty or in want.
>
> —PHILIPPIANS 4:11–12

What a testimony of faith! Like Abraham, Paul knew the Lord as his Jehovah Jireh—his provider. He saw the circumstances in his life from an eternal perspective. He had an unshakable faith in the Person of Jesus Christ. And he knew the abundance of God's grace, that God loved him so much He would always sustain him.

Paul and Abraham show us that we don't need to be afraid. When our "treasure" is with God, with faith in Him, this world can do nothing to truly harm us. We are reassured in this life by our knowledge and belief in eternal life in the Person of Jesus Christ. We belong to the Creator, Redeemer, and Sustainer of the universe. We are His children and He will protect us and provide for us. We don't need to worry. We have nothing to fear. The Lord will take care of us now and for eternity.

Grace

Why does God love such selfish, rebellious, independent people as you and me? Why does He love us even though we worry and fret and complain?—because of His grace. This grace is totally undeserved. We haven't done, and we never will do, anything to earn it. We can never show that we have earned His grace. We can only show that we don't deserve it.

> For it is by grace you have been saved, through faith—and this not from yourselves, it is the gift of God—not by works, so that no one can boast.
>
> —EPHESIANS 2:8–9

The Scriptures define grace as God's favor, His undeserved kindness bestowed on our lives. When we receive salvation through Christ, we are receiving the grace of God and enjoying His divine favor on our lives. The apostle Paul declared of himself: "But by the grace of God I am what I am" (1 Cor. 15:10). By the grace of God, we are what we are. It is by His grace that we are saved. Everything is done by the grace of God, and by the grace of God we allow others to be who they are. We just have to get it through our heads, our hearts, our pride, and our sense of self-importance that His grace allows Him to love us and provide for us beyond our understanding.

Our actions and accomplishments do not save us; trusting in the Person of Christ and the cross saves us. Praise God for His grace! For if we were treated fairly, if we were given what we deserved, none of us would be spending eternity with our Creator, Redeemer, and Sustainer.

Humility is developed in our lives when we acknowledge the grace of God that we have received. In fact, we must humble ourselves in order to receive His grace. It is the proud heart that does not seek to know God, according to the Scriptures:

> In his pride the wicked does not seek him; in all his thoughts there is no room for God.
>
> —PSALM 10:4

As we humble our hearts to admit our need of God, He manifests to us His grace and love and gives us His divine presence. Then our hearts are filled with awe and gratitude for this loving God who forgives our sin and gives us His peace and all we need for life. His love causes us to bow in worship before His throne of grace and to express our deep appreciation of who He is and what He has done for us.

All worry and fear are knocked out when we believe in this grace. When we believe God's grace to be the ruling aspect of our lives, fear and worry leave. When grace is present, we surrender to His will and feel His firm fingers of control over our lives.

We're filled with joy because we know we're with Him forever and He will provide for us forever. We realize the power of the resurrection is ours for eternity. Author John Piper calls it "future grace"—grace which is ours not just after our entrance into heaven, but which fills each moment as God provides for us.[4] His grace is sufficient for today, tomorrow, and eternity.

We can use our faith in His future grace to battle worry in practical ways. John Piper, who pastors Bethlehem Baptist

Church in Minneapolis, encourages us to look to God's promises in His Word when fear and anxiety try to take hold in our lives. He will intervene. He will help us. He will sustain us. He will give us fresh courage and faith. Here are some examples of God's promises that Rev. Piper references in his book, *Future Grace*:

When we're anxious about a new situation and *fear the unknown*:

> So do not fear, for I am with you; do not be dismayed, for I am your God. I will strengthen you and help you; I will uphold you with my righteous right hand.
>
> —ISAIAH 41:10

When we're anxious about our efforts to serve God and we *feel useless* and empty:

> So is my word that goes out from my mouth: It will not return to me empty, but will accomplish what I desire and achieve the purpose for which I sent it.
>
> —ISAIAH 55:11

When we're anxious about the weaknesses we feel in our lives:

> My grace is sufficient for you, for my power is made perfect in weakness.
>
> 2 CORINTHIANS 12:9

When we're anxious about decisions that will affect our future:

> I will instruct you and teach you in the way you should go; I will counsel you and watch over you.
>
> —PSALM 32:8

When we face opposition:

> If God is for us, who can be against us?
>
> —ROMANS 8:31

R̥ for Worry

When we're anxious about the welfare of *family and friends*, we can remember that God is our Father and knows how to give good things to His children:

> If you, then, though you are evil, know how to give good gifts to your children, how much more will your Father in heaven give good gifts to those who ask him!
>
> —MATTHEW 7:11

When we're anxious about being sick:

> A righteous man may have many troubles, but the LORD delivers him from them all.
>
> —PSALM 34:19

When we're anxious about *aging* and getting old:

> Even to your old age and gray hairs I am he, I am he who will sustain you.
>
> —ISAIAH 46:4

Future grace doesn't just keep us from needing to worry—it demolishes worry! The beauty of God's future grace is that it will be sufficient not only now, but for eternity. We are His forever. His provision is forever. God gives us future grace with such hope that nothing else should cause us to worry today. We're intertwined and engulfed with Him forever and He'll provide for us forever. His Word will reassure us of His promises and strengthen our belief in His future grace. If we don't realize the beauty of God's future grace to take care of us forever, we fail to realize the purpose of the creation and our purpose in living. That purpose is to live our lives in peace, to glorify God, and enjoy Him forever because we rest in His grace.

Thanksgiving

Banks Anderson, a doctor in ophthalmology at Duke, was once asked, "If you had only one choice of medicine, what would you take?" He said, "Corticosteriods, of course. They can treat many ophthalmologic diseases; more than any other medicine." Corticosteriods can knock down inflammation and treat more diseases than any antibiotic or immunosuppressant agent.

As I consider the therapy for worry, I think of the best medicine for it—a thanksgiving frenzy to the Lord. This lavish expression of thanksgiving is more than something we do at meals, birthdays, and holidays. It's a mental attitude of continual thanks to God that permeates our thoughts and lives. It engulfs our relationship with God, our relationships with others, and our relationship to our vocation. Expressing our gratitude and thanksgiving is a daily necessity in the war against worry. The apostle Paul tells us how important thanksgiving is:

> Rejoice in the Lord always. I will say it again: Rejoice! Let your gentleness be evident to all. The Lord is near. Do not be anxious about anything, but in everything, by prayer and petition, with thanksgiving, present your requests to God. And the peace of God, which transcends all understanding, will guard your hearts and your minds in Christ Jesus.
>
> —PHILIPPIANS 4:4–7

Paul is talking about a habit and lifestyle of thanksgiving—a thanksgiving frenzy. He tells us we are to give thanks in all things. We are to be prayerful in all things. The two really fit together. Because when we give thanks, we are thankful to our Creator, our God. We pray prayers of thanksgiving.

Cultivating a spirit of thanksgiving is not optional for believers. If we are to experience a true relationship with God, we must be thankful to Him. We're thankful for the grace that saves us from our sins. We overflow with thanksgiving for the Person of Jesus Christ living in us. He takes away our sin and accepts our repentance. We express our wonder and awe for His eternal love in our lives as we worship and adore Him as our sovereign Lord.

R for Worry

A thankful heart is the basis of a healthy heart—a heart that is holding onto Him. We must be thankful for God's grace—His future grace and His past grace, as well as His present grace. We have the hope of future grace of being intertwined with Him for eternity. What joy we will have being with Him and our loved ones for eternity! It's this joy that changes our lives in the present. It's this thankfulness for our future that keeps us walking in the Spirit, surrendered to God's will for our lives. His past grace in our lives reveals His great faithfulness to us. And His present grace reveals His sovereignty over our lives, which makes us secure in His love, resting in His redemption. And His future grace fills us with hope, promising an eternity of bliss with Him.

Being thankful to Him delivers us from despair. Being thankful to Him delivers us from being perplexed and crushed. Being thankful to Him gives us a joyous, happy, and overcoming heart. We're thankful from the top of our heads to the bottom of our feet. We can praise the Lord in the midst of difficult times because we have seen His blessings in the good times. We can ask God, listen to Him, pray for deliverance, and seek His wisdom.

Some of us say the words "thank you" so often that they become a part of us. Others are quiet and express "thank you" with a touch, a look, an attitude of care and concern—understanding and appreciating without words. We're all different, and rightfully so. But each of us must express our spirit of thanksgiving.

Luke describes how one man demonstrated the thankful spirit:

> Now on his way to Jerusalem, Jesus traveled along the border between Samaria and Galilee. As he was going into a village, ten men who had leprosy met him. They stood at a distance and called out in a loud voice, "Jesus, Master, have pity on us!"

When he saw them, he said, "Go, show yourselves to
the priests." And as they went, they were cleansed.

One of them, when he saw he was healed, came back,
praising God in a loud voice. He threw himself at Jesus'
feet and thanked him—and he was a Samaritan.

Jesus asked, "Were not all ten cleansed? Where are the
other nine? Was no one found to return and give praise to
God except this foreigner?" Then he said to him, "Rise and
go; your faith has made you well."

—LUKE 17:11–19

One man came back to Jesus in thanksgiving. Only one
related to Him. Only one became personal with Christ. This is
the thankful state each of us should have. As believers, we must
give ourselves to God in thanksgiving and live on a person-to-
Person basis with Him, because the Holy Spirit lives within us.
Our thanksgiving frenzy aligns us to God. And the more closely
aligned we are in our relationship with God, the less place we
have in our lives for worry. Thanksgiving displaces worry and
anxiety.

Being thankful helps us to realize who God is and who we are.
We stand in gratitude because of His constant forgiveness of our
sins and rebellion against Him. Indeed, we cannot give thanks
until we realize that we are nothing on our own, yet everything
through Him. We know His future grace, His present grace, and
His past grace will take care of us. It is truly impossible to worry
if we are living a lifestyle of thanksgiving frenzy.

Through Jesus, therefore, let us continually offer to God a
sacrifice of praise—the fruit of lips that confess his name.

—HEBREWS 13:15

It is impossible to be anxious if we are cultivating a grateful heart. In thanksgiving, we are focused on God in the Person of Jesus Christ, and we're thankful for everything we
have. Thanksgiving banishes selfishness—the seeds of worry.

R̤ *for* Worry

We triumph over a selfish mind-set when we are continually thankful to God for being our Provider now and forever. This eternal view puts worry into its proper perspective. A thanksgiving frenzy lifts our life above the cares of this world. We know what is real, lasting, and true. We are thankful to God for His presence and the promise of eternity with Him. Thanksgiving gives us the peace of God rather than the anxiety and fear generated by the concerns of this world.

A thankful spirit extends beyond our relationship with God. It also strengthens our relationships with our loved ones. A thankful spirit is so essential in many relationships, especially that of marriage. Steadfast thankfulness produces strength, support, and growth in marriage. Continuous gestures of love, support, and thanks give our spouse a sense of self-worth; they build a relationship of trust and love.

In the same way, we need to be thankful for other friends, family, and co-workers—all those with whom we rub shoulders in our daily lives. We can serve, we can give, we can be partners, and we can love others when we have a genuine spirit of thanksgiving for them.

As followers of Christ, this spirit must be the essence of everything we do. In every activity, whether it's doing delicate surgery, writing books, presenting a legal defense, or sweeping a hall, we must have an attitude of thanksgiving.

> Give thanks to the LORD, call on his name; make known among the nations what he has done. Sing to him, sing praise to him; tell of all his wonderful acts. Glory in his holy name; let the hearts of those who seek the LORD rejoice. Look to the LORD and his strength; seek his face always.
>
> —PSALM 105:1–4

My only really outstanding athletic achievement was a Double Ironman Triathlon in which I finished about one minute behind the first American competitor in the event. At the time,

I was 56, and he was 28. Both of us did very well. But what's interesting is that for me, the most important thing I did was to stay in an attitude of thanksgiving during the whole race.

In that race I never had the up and down emotional cycles most athletes usually face in long competitions. Instead, I concentrated on reciting Bible verses and being thankful. I never really struggled mentally. The attitude of thanksgiving permeated everything I did during that race.

Being thankful moves our faith to rest in His grace. Faith, grace, and thanksgiving, embodied in the Person of Jesus Christ, take away our need to worry and allow us to be engulfed by the presence of God—now and for eternity. That is the ultimate antidote for worry!

Thanksgiving and Laughter

We can take thanksgiving one step further. When we're filled with thanksgiving, we're joyful. It's impossible to be gloomy and depressed when our hearts are full of thanksgiving to God. This thanksgiving frenzy manifests itself in a way we don't always consider: laughing.

How long has it been since you had a good belly laugh? Good laughter seems to be a treasure that is in short supply. It is one of the gifts of being human, and it is an essential ingredient in life. Many times as we try to clear our minds of different thoughts, desires, and wants, we should just simply look at the situation and start laughing. Laughter, particularly as we laugh at ourselves in the situation, will clear our minds.

My friend Spencer Thornton and I talk about the changes that laughter brings. A laughter frenzy will clear our minds when they're bogged down in worry. And it increases our endorphin level. We need to just let go and really laugh our worries off. Spencer, an ophthalmologist, has also been an actor and performer. He helps me try to "do a laugh" in the mornings. He goes through this laughing routine, making himself go "Ha, ha, ha, ha, ha!" to get his body tuned for laughing.

And Spencer should know about laughter. He and his wife have both had to fight severe problems with cancer. He has shown me that laughter changes the way we focus on our presence in the world.

Someone may think this kind of laughter is a false laughter. But it's really therapeutic laughter. It's wonderful to start the day thinking about laughing and how important it is to laugh—and to laugh often! Laughter can permeate our souls so we're no longer dark and negative people. When we laugh, we perceive ourselves differently and we're radiant and bright. This internal joy shows in our actions and behavior.

Monkeys get serious when they itch. We may wonder why they don't laugh and have joy. There is a part of laughter that comes from joy and happiness. It's so important that we have the true joy of God within our hearts and that it's expressed in laughter. We must laugh with joy in His presence. Because if we don't have joy, we aren't expressing true Christianity, and we're turning away many people.

Discussion Questions

1. What does faith mean to you? How do you see faith at work in your daily life?

   _____

   _____

   _____

2. What does grace mean to you? List some ways you sense God's grace.

   _____

   _____

3. What does thanksgiving mean to you? When do you feel most thankful? Least thankful? List five ways you can be more thankful. Practice at least one way every day this week.

_____

_____

_____

4. Try having a good laugh first thing in the morning. Does it change your outlook on the day?

_____

_____

_____

For further reflection

> For it is by grace you have been saved, through faith—and this not from yourselves, it is the gift of God—not by works, so that no one can boast.
>
> —EPHESIANS 2:8–9

Faith and grace work together to bring us thanksgiving in the Lord. How do these three work in your life? Describe some ways you can focus on them to change the way you live your life.

Chapter 10

BIRTH INTO
the KINGDOM of GOD

EOPLE WILL DO anything to preserve life. Think about all the advertisements on television, in magazines, and in newspapers for ways to live longer and look younger. Yet, according to the Scriptures, there's only one way to eternal life and that's found in the Person of Jesus Christ.

Life truly begins when we believe what Christ accomplished at Calvary, where He gave His life for you and me. At the moment we accept Christ's provision for our sin, we're no longer simply preserving our temporal lives; we're born into the kingdom of God through Christ. The forgiveness of sins, the grace of God, and the hope of eternity with God all become ours at that moment of placing true faith in our Savior, Jesus Christ. We admit that we've been independent and rebellious. And we ask His forgiveness for being selfish and self-centered. We say, "Lord, I'm sorry for being so willful. I'm ready to be focused on You now. I ask You to work through me." In an attitude of repentance, we hand over the reins of our life to His will and direction. And we begin our journey to complete transformation through trust in Christ as our faithful and sovereign Lord and Savior.

At the Alamo, Col. William B. Travis asked men to cross the line to give themselves in defending the provisional government in San Antonio as it sought Texas' independence from Mexico. That call came at great personal cost. All two hundred defenders died at the Alamo.[1]

At salvation, Christ asks all of us to cross the line—to give ourselves to Him. He asks us to put aside our own agendas and desires, and to submit our lives to Him. We are not first called to "do" but to *surrender to the lordship of Christ.*

The Alamo was a turning point in American history. Each of us faces a personal turning point when we respond to Christ. He summons; we must respond. He tells us we will face this choice:

> No one can serve two masters. Either he will hate the one and love the other, or he will be devoted to the one and despise the other. You cannot serve both God and Money.
>
> —MATTHEW 6:24

Jesus says we must decide whom we are going to serve. He demands that we make a choice. Do we say yes to Jesus Christ, who loves us and gave Himself on the cross for us? It's not a decision to be taken lightly. Saying yes means total commitment—that we love Him with our heart, mind, soul, and strength, and that we act out that love every day in faith and thanksgiving. Paul describes our commitment this way:

> Therefore, I urge you, brothers, in view of God's mercy, to offer your bodies as living sacrifices, holy and pleasing to God—this is your spiritual act of worship. Do not conform any longer to the pattern of this world, but be transformed by the renewing of your mind.
>
> —ROMANS 12:1–2

The Scriptures teach that worship is not merely an external expression of thanksgiving and praise to God; it is best expressed through complete surrender to His lordship over our lives. Christianity is nothing but the Person of Jesus—His miracle of birth, His life, His death to take care of our sins, and His amazing resurrection that gives us eternal life and fellowship with Him. In the Person of Christ all things are centered and all things revolve. What He asks of us is to change our focus. He calls us to repent of our selfishness and worldly desires and to embrace His transforming power.

Christ asks us to follow Him in the same attitude of humility He demonstrated when He came to earth:

> Who, being in very nature God, did not consider equality with God something to be grasped, but made himself nothing, taking the very nature of a servant, being made in human likeness. And being found in appearance as a man, he humbled himself and became obedient to death— even death on a cross! Therefore God exalted him to the highest place and gave him the name that is above every name, that at the name of Jesus every knee should bow, in heaven and on earth and under the earth, and every tongue confess that Jesus Christ is Lord, to the glory of God the Father.
>
> —PHILIPPIANS 2:6–11

When we say yes to the Person of Jesus Christ, completely and without reservation, the eternal kingdom of God is born in us. We are His children. We are cleansed and refreshed by Him, beginning now and lasting through eternity. And we begin a journey toward a life filled with joy when are born into the kingdom of God, surrendering our lives wholeheartedly to God.

Once we experience the satisfying presence of God in our lives through our surrender to Christ's lordship, we discover that He is the source of ultimate joy. I have considered three critical steps in our journey to a joy-filled life: *grace, relinquishment,* and *faith.* When we truly appreciate God's grace, we cannot help but relinquish everything to Him in faith in His goodness. I believe joy is a result of that natural outpouring of our hearts in every relationship and situation of life as we surrender to God's presence in our lives.

As children in the kingdom of God, our attitude can no longer be that of the world, but of His kingdom. We begin to see life differently. We no longer seek satisfaction and fulfillment in the things of this world. We have an ever-growing measure of satisfaction now and forever in God, through the Person of Jesus Christ.

We have the eternal perspective that we talked about earlier.

Surrendering to God separates us from much of the thinking of the world. We have a brand new outlook, a brand new life, and an eternal faith in our eternal Father.

We no longer have faith in the world, which is based on the immediate, the seen, and the now. Instead, we have faith in God—eternal faith, based on the promise of Christ and our Father to provide for us now and forever. It is not faith based on a weak human emotion. It is faith focused on God's power, love, and grace. As we learn to trust His faithfulness and sovereign rule over all, our hearts are filled with great joy. And that joy leads to ever-deeper worship and adoration as we bow in humility in the presence of our Lord.

This life goes by very quickly. Many who are in their 40s think the past twenty years have gone by too quickly. Those in their 60s think the past twenty years have gone even faster. However, when we live with God's perspective, we see time simply as the preamble to eternity. We're cared for now and we're cared for forever.

We see God as our Father and provider, our Jehovah Jireh. As a father, I have wanted very much to provide for my children. I really haven't cared much for my own circumstances and possessions, but I have always wanted to make sure my children were taken care of. And now that I'm a grandfather, I feel that desire even more. This is the same way the Lord looks at us. He wants to make sure we're provided for. And because He's God, He can meet all our needs—now and for eternity.

As His children, we can say, "Lord, let us find our place with You for eternity and let that take away all the anxieties." Knowing and believing in eternal life in Jesus Christ gives us hope and freedom in this world.

> It is for freedom that Christ has set us free. Stand firm, then, and do not let yourselves be burdened again by a yoke of slavery.
>
> —GALATIANS 5:1

All of us worry about one thing or another. Until we learn to surrender to Christ daily, our own efforts at squashing fear and worry will fail. But when we surrender to God, we refuse to surrender to worry and the slavery it creates. His grace frees us from fear. He has taken responsibility for looking out for us. No matter how difficult life might seem today, we are in His kingdom forever. We have died to self; we live in the kingdom of God.

> Therefore, since we are receiving a kingdom that cannot be shaken, let us be thankful.
> —HEBREWS 12:28

God's kingdom is eternal and everlasting. Our thanksgiving for His future grace destroys worry! And our gratitude for His past and present grace fills our hearts with worship and adoration for our Redeemer. He will help us in our daily commitment to living a life of thanksgiving and surrender. He will provide the support we need in tough times. He will be our constant companion. God, the Author of the universe, promises He will abide with us in this process of surrender and transformation.

> I can do everything through him who gives me strength.
> —PHILIPPIANS 4:13

Our own strength is never sufficient. Our feeble, fallible, human efforts will fail, and we will fall victim to all forms of selfishness and worry, anxiety and fear, and pride and control. Only through Christ can we be transformed to live a life of surrender. We must be completely honest with ourselves and realize Christ is all; we are nothing.

> Unless the LORD builds the house, its builders labor in vain.
> —PSALM 127:1

We must look to Christ. None of us can do it alone. Jesus will perfect us; He will mature us; He will transform us. He will continue to work in our lives until we see Him face to face.

> Being confident of this, that he who began a good work in you will carry it on to completion until the day of Christ Jesus.
>
> —PHILIPPIANS 1:6

As believers who have received salvation through Christ, God has begun a work in us, and He will see it through. We need to be able to say: "God, I thank You that You began a good work in me. I thank You that, no matter how unfinished I am at the moment, You will gloriously complete Your work on the day of Christ Jesus. Heavenly Father, help me to cooperate with You as You mold me into the likeness of Jesus. Amen."

We say with Paul, "I can do all things through Christ who strengthens me" (Phil. 4:13, NKJV). We can do all things because we have the spiritual strength of knowing that God's sovereign power has control over all eternity. We have faith to conquer fears. We have exceeding gratitude that will vanquish worries. And we have His peace and His power, enabling us in all areas of life.

True peace is not passive; it's an active, equipping power to do the work of God. Transformation is not just an internal process. It also demands an external response. In the next chapter, let's look at how we can live that courageous life of faith, thanksgiving, and grace.

Discussion Questions

1. Have you crossed the line to commit your life to Jesus? If not, are you willing to do so now?

_____

_____

_____

2. List some ways Jesus has changed you since you surrendered yourself to Him.

_____

_____

_____

3. How much have you grasped of the three essential elements of your journey toward a life of joy: grace, relinquishment, faith?

_____

_____

_____

4. How do you sense Christ's presence in your life? How are you aware of His transforming power in your life now? Keep a journal this week recording the ways you realize His presence.

_____

_____

_____

5. What steps do you need to take to fully rest, without fear, in the hands of Jesus?

_____

_____

_____

For further reflection

For God so loved the world that he gave his one and only Son, that whoever believes in him shall not perish but have eternal life.

—JOHN 3:16

When we believe in the finished work of Christ, we are given eternal life through Him. Discuss how you recognize His eternity in your life.

Chapter 11

COURAGEOUS FAITH

BEING RECKLESS CAUSES worry. Reckless investors worry. Reckless fantasies and reckless sexuality cause worry. Therefore it's vital to be careful. Actually, being a Christian is the most conservative and safe lifestyle we can live. If we love God and don't worry, we adopt the safest lifestyle possible.

Conversely, one must be a little reckless in order to do well. When instructors teach skiing, they say, "You have to be a bit of a fool to be a good skier." When the instructor says to be a little foolish, he's not telling us to go and break a leg (as I've done). He's telling us to relax and not worry too much. Otherwise we can't get the truly great feeling of skiing.

In other words, we can't be overly anxious. We have to free ourselves from worries about every little concern. We have to be a little bit of a fool. A person who is free of the obsessions of worry is able to do a good job—and enjoys every area of life.

When we're totally relaxed in skiing, we can do something called "anticipation," which is just dropping down on the lower ski and letting the rebound phenomenon carry us around into a turn. It is almost effortless to do mid-turns as we get the motion down. The more we relax, the more effortless skiing becomes.

This is true in daily life as well. Worry keeps us from being courageous in our families and friendships and in our service to God. If we will just relax and come back to the basics of a simpler life, the normal routine will take care of us. In the spiritual life, if we go back to the basics of faith and trust, life becomes easy, as skiing becomes easy.

We learn to drop down in anticipation in a ski maneuver that makes skiing effortless. In life, we drop down on our knees in prayer and commit our lives to Christ, turning everything over to Him. Then, when we stand up, the run (either on the ski slope or in life) is smoother. There's very little effort. No pushing, shoving, or twisting. Both allow us to perform our runs in a smoother, easier, more tranquil way, with less energy, less worry, and less effort.

When we decide we can do with less, and material things really aren't important to us, we demonstrate our faith in Jehovah Jireh, the God who provides.

> Be strong and courageous. Do not be afraid or terrified because of them, for the LORD your God goes with you; he will never leave you nor forsake you.
>
> —DEUTERONOMY 31:6

Faith says we don't have to focus on ourselves and on our possessions. Faith says we don't need to acquire an abundance. Faith says we don't have to own more than other people. Faith says we are filled with God's presence and that is sufficient for us. Out of that faith comes the ability to love, because faith works through love and love works through faith. Then we are as a flowing river, a wellspring of life. What's inside us—the joy that's in the Lord—manifests itself as a smooth, even flow of love out of us.

Giving Courageously

When we are generous, we are actually waging spiritual warfare. What we really are doing is fighting with mammon and laughing in the face of mammon. When we give away money and possessions that other people would hoard, we are simply saying God is our supplier and we can give away what we need to give away.

When we appreciate and esteem others as Christ teaches us to do, we will find ways to give to them out of our material resources as well as out of our affections. Courageous faith is a giving faith:

> What good is it, my brothers, if a man claims to have
> faith but has no deeds? Can such faith save him? Suppose
> a brother or sister is without clothes and daily food. If
> one of you says to him, "Go, I wish you well; keep warm
> and well fed," but does nothing about his physical needs,
> what good is it? In the same way, faith by itself, if it is not
> accompanied by action, is dead.
>
> —JAMES 2:14–17

Jesus taught us about giving generously and offering hos-
pitality when He miraculously fed five thousand men from
five loaves of bread and two fish. (See Luke 9:10–17.) As was
true so many times during His ministry on earth, a crowd had
gathered around Jesus. After a while, the people got hungry.
The disciples weren't sure what to do, but Jesus had a plan to
demonstrate His generous spirit: "You give them something to
eat," He said (Luke 9:13). All the disciples could find were the
fish and bread; Jesus prayed to give thanks and it was multiplied to feed the multitude. The message is clear: Do what you
can with what you have, giving thanks, and He will provide
more. And Jesus teaches that we must look to heaven to get
our fill of physical as well as spiritual food. The Scriptures con-
demn selfish greed, which is the opposite of generosity:

> I have seen a grievous evil under the sun: wealth hoarded
> to the harm of its owner, or wealth lost through some mis-
> fortune, so that when he has a son there is nothing left for
> him.
>
> —ECCLESIASTES 5:13–14

If we worry about keeping our money and our possessions,
they will do us no good, and we can't use them to benefit others. On the other hand, I know many people who give more
than they earn many years, drawing from reserves. We must
be givers whose inward being is thankful for what we have and
who want to share with others. A giving heart is one that truly

appreciates God and our fellowman and expresses that appreciation through its generosity.

Many people come to us wanting funds. It's important for us to give from our hearts. We are good stewards when we give with the joy of the Lord in our hearts. We can't give solely out of a sense of duty or out of guilt. We can't give if it only makes us feel proud of ourselves or builds us up. We can genuinely give only when we feel that God has anointed it.

It's also important to evaluate where to give our money. Just as we are good stewards in giving, we must make sure our gifts go to those who are good stewards. We should give to those organizations and individuals where the money will be most efficiently used for the Lord's work, to the greatest benefit, both now and throughout the ensuing years. As we decide where to give our money, we must try to ascertain that Jesus Christ is the center of any ministry we consider. Money should be given with a great deal of discernment and prayer in focusing on the Person of Jesus Christ.

Our uneasiness about giving money goes away when we have faith that God will be our provider and we're thankful for all He has given us. Our uneasiness about how those gifts will be used goes away when we listen to the Holy Spirit about where and when to give. When we can give without anxiety, we exhibit the grace of God within our lives, and others will see the difference that God's love makes in us. Our trust in God's sovereignty and in His faithfulness helps us to follow His direction in all of our giving.

Loving Courageously

Love is defined and described by various terms. There's a three-letter s-word that everybody knows: sex. There's a six-letter s-word that few people know, and very few understand: *storge* (pronounced stor–gay). C. S. Lewis describes it in his book, *The Four Loves*.[1]

Now, there are many kinds of love. Lewis wrote about four.

Philos is the love among friends. *Eros* is the love between man and woman. *Agape* is the love God has for us and the love we have for Him. The love experience with our friends and family helps us to understand the love of God.

The fourth love is the s-word: *storge*, which is affection. According to Lewis, it's like glue holding the other three loves together. This affection is the humblest love—a love without airs. It binds us together. When it enters into the other loves, it is the very medium by which they operate from day to day.

Storge relates to our attitude of thanksgiving. As Lewis discusses *storge*, he also seems to describe it as "appreciation."[2]" "In my experience," writes Lewis, "it is affection that creates a [wide] taste [in humanity], teaching us first to notice, then to endure, then to smile at, then to enjoy, and finally to appreciate, the people who 'happen to be there.'"[3]

The Scriptures teach us to "love [our] neighbor as [ourselves.]" We must learn to appreciate others being as special to God as we are. Affection will help us to fulfill the biblical instruction: "In lowliness of mind let each esteem others better than himself" (Phil. 2:3, NKJV).

We can't have a constant attitude of thanksgiving without affection and appreciation. We appreciate the Lord, not just for everything He does for us, but also for who He is and so we live in thanks for Him. And that thanksgiving leads to a real, intrinsic love relationship with God, which is our internal response to our surrender to Him.

All the other forms of love create the framework in which *agape*—God's love—can be expressed. Those loves weave together to create a symphony of life leading us to eternal bliss with God.

> And so we know and rely on the love God has for us. God is love. Whoever lives in love lives in God, and God in him.
>
> —1 JOHN 4:16

When we surrender our lives to God, we enter into an intimate relationship with Him. This is not a mental relationship in which we may know and respect Christ. It goes deeper than that. We are actually in love with Christ! And we begin to grow in grace to maturely live our faith and express our love.

Storge also affects the way we live out our love for others. It shouldn't be misunderstood as being the other loves; we appreciate, respect, care for, and encourage others through *storge*. This kind affection transforms our relationships with others. No longer are we worried about what we can do for ourselves. *Storge* helps us focus on what we can do for others. At St. Luke's Cataract and Laser Institute, our job is to encourage our patients and their family members. In society, in all our relationships, we must show respect, we must encourage, and we must care for one another.

Appreciation makes life meaningful because it creates meaningful relationships. No longer are we selfish. We genuinely care for others first. That includes serving others, appreciating others, and encouraging others. It also includes relieving others' anxieties. When we concern ourselves with their concerns and fears and worries, we do two things. First, we help them share their burdens and decrease their fears. Second, we take the focus off ourselves and put it on others in a Christ-like fashion. We are living examples of *storge*—genuine affection and appreciation for others.

This sincerity of appreciation constitutes the importance of relationships. We must build up relationships with others because those relationships are one of life's most beautiful blessings. The hectic pace of life can pull us back to a worldly view. We need relationships with others built on God's love to keep us focused on loving Him and seeking His will. The lack of appreciation makes us revert back to a life of selfishness, which leads us back to worry. But God's Word tells us that love (which would include *storge*) gives us peace.

Perfect love drives out fear.

—1 JOHN 4:18

Love is always sacrificial. Our *agape* love for God, as well as our love for friends and family, is realistic, sacrificial, purposeful, willing, and absolute. As God guides us in love, we guide each other. Our response to God's love is to love others, respecting them, offering consistent appreciation for who they are and what they do, and helping them to grow in love. We should all seek relationships of mutual encouragement.

Serving Courageously

For even the Son of Man did not come to be served, but to serve, and to give his life as a ransom for many.

—MARK 10:45

One of the greatest roles in life is that of a caregiver and a servant. This expression of love embodies *storge*. Many physicians I've talked with can't wait to retire. I never want to quit! I want to be a caregiver for the rest of my life. I see many nurses who feel as I do, as well as many other people who, regardless of their current occupation, just want to be a servant to others for the rest of their lives.

Jesus is the role model for service. He is the perfect servant and the perfect caregiver. At home I have a statue of Him washing the feet of His disciples. It helps me remember His service and shows me how I can follow in His steps.

In our relationships we must remember to give, not to take. Being a caregiver keeps us from selfishness, and the worries and fears that result. Giving to others makes us stronger people and strengthens our relationships with others.

We are never happy if we desire to be served and lifted up and pampered. We're worried about how others can take care of us and meet our needs. We're selfish and that always leads to worry and anxiety. I had an aunt who stayed in bed until 10:00

a.m. every day. She always wanted to be pampered. She always wanted more, and she was never satisfied. She had the nicest husband in the world; he gave her everything. But I don't think she ever appreciated him. She just ended up dissipating and dying without ever finding satisfaction and the beautiful feeling of enjoying a life of work and service.

On the other hand, there's the story of a couple that chose a loving resolution regarding their differing preferences for morning coffee. The husband liked regular coffee. The wife liked flavored coffee. In their marriage, when the husband awoke first, he made flavored coffee. When the wife awoke first, she made regular coffee. Simple gestures of love and caregiving have a great effect on our relationships.

When I see patients, I thank them for letting me be their caregiver. This lets them know that I care for them. I don't want to be just their physician; I want to be their caregiver. I want to be a servant to them. Each of us should strive to be thankful servants in our lives. There is no greater reward from work than thankful service and caregiving.

Several of us at St. Luke's Cataract and Laser Institute have committed ourselves to recite the thirteenth chapter of 1 Corinthians each day. We want to focus on what is so easy to miss in our daily lives—loving the Lord and loving others. The following is a paraphrase of this chapter, substituting words related to "caregiving" for "love" and adding some thoughts—showing love as it meets the road of reality:

> If I speak in the tongues of men and of angels, but have not a caregiver's heart, I am only a resounding gong or a clanging cymbal. Therefore, if I talk about things that are important in medicine, theology and science, but really don't care for people, I'm pretty hollow.
>
> If I have the gift of prophecy and can fathom all mysteries and all knowledge, and if I have a faith that can move mountains, but have not a caregiver's heart, I am

nothing. In other words, I can be smart and biblical, having been saved by grace through faith, but if I don't have a caregiver's heart, I'm nothing.

If I give all I possess to the poor and surrender my body to the flames, but am not a caregiver, I gain nothing. I can be generous to others and give sacrificially, but unless my heart is full of godly love, and I am caring for others, I've missed my ministry in Christ—for me to focus on Him and, as a result, be a caregiver.

Caregiving is patient (How I wish I were more patient!), caregiving is kind. Caregiving does not envy other people's caregiving or anything else. Envy and covetousness destroy our relationship with God. He is most satisfied with us when we are most satisfied with Him. Caregiving does not boast of caregiving or anything else. Whatever comes, comes…and is taken as a matter of fact. Caregivers care because they love Jesus. Caregiving is not proud. Caregiving is humble. The true caregiver doesn't give care for recognition, but cares because his heart has been changed toward Christ, and he delights in the ministry of caregiving.

Caregiving is not rude. It does not interrupt. Caregiving is not self-seeking. It is not done for the benefits the caregiver receives. A caregiver is not easily angered. A caregiver keeps no record of wrongs. The caregiver keeps focused on God's grace, His love, His Person—and as a result, becomes a caregiver.

A caregiver does not delight in evil but rejoices with the truth, which is God's love, His life, His light, and His Son.

Caregiving always protects, always trusts. A caregiver always looks at the best in others and can be depended upon. A caregiver always hopes for the best and always perseveres in the caregiving. For example, the Good Samaritan [see Luke 10:25–37] gave freely of his time and money. He was greater than the priest and the Levite who were interested in their positions and did not care.

Caregiving never fails. But where there are prophecies and wisdoms, they will cease; where there are tongues and great orations and talks, they will be stilled; where there is great medical and theological knowledge, it will pass away quickly.

For we know in part, we know a little bit about what is involved in caring for patients and others, and we guess what may come in the future, but when perfection comes, when Christ comes, the imperfect disappears.

When I was a child, throughout my pilgrimage on earth learning to be a better caregiver, I talked like a child, I thought like a child, I reasoned like a child. When I became a man, when I became truly mature, I put childish ways behind me (though those closest to me may not see it sometimes).

Now we see but a poor reflection as in a mirror of the things that are going to come; then we shall see the Lord face to face. Now I know in part about God and theology from the Bible; then I shall know fully, and that is full intimacy, even as I am fully known. As a Christian, I seek God's intimacy more than anything. I need God's intimacy to be a caregiver.

And now these three remain: faith, hope, and caregiving. But the greatest of these is caregiving. It changes us first on the inside and then on the outside. Faith works through love, and hope results from it. Caregiving is the love we show to others in our families, in our social relationships, and in our profession of medicine.

May each of us follow the way of caregiving and eagerly desire spiritual gifts—especially the gift of godly wisdom.

Caregiving is the ultimate expression of love, appreciation, and encouragement. It's the greatest result of *storge* mixing with the other loves of our lives, changing our focus and our attitudes, taking us from selfishness to sacrifice. When we appreciate others enough to serve them in genuine love and care, we don't have time to worry. When we focus on the needs of others, our own selfish needs and desires fade away. We are satisfied in our relationship with God, who promised to meet all our needs (see Phil. 4:19). And we are filled with the joy of serving God's people as He directed us to do.

As we learn to trust in God's future grace, preparing us for eternity with Him, we are transformed inside and out. This transformation enables us to appreciate God for who He truly is—our constant provider, our agent of change, our Lord and Redeemer, and Heavenly Friend. Amen.

Discussion Questions

1. List some ways you can live a life of courageous faith this week.

   _____

   _____

   _____

   _____

   _____

2. What keeps you from courageously giving of yourself?

   _____

   _____

   _____

   _____

3. Apply *storge* to your relationships with others. How does it change them?

_____

_____

_____

_____

4. Do you know caregivers? Ask them why they serve others.

_____

_____

_____

_____

For further reflection

> Give, and it will be given to you. A good measure, pressed down, shaken together and running over, will be poured into your lap. For with the measure you use, it will be measured to you.
>
> —LUKE 6:38

We must have an attitude of giving. When we give, we make our life doubly meaningful. What are some ways you can give and serve?

Chapter 12

GROWING in GOD

W HEN I WAS ten years old, I worried plenty. I worried about what junior high school would be like. I compared myself with my father, who had succeeded in many ways, and I worried that I would never be as successful as he was. I worried that girls didn't like me as much as they liked other ten-year-old boys. I worried about what my teachers would think of my grades. I worried about being accepted by the other kids on my street.

At age twenty, I worried about how I would do in college, about what kind of athlete I would be, about whether I would be accepted by others—especially girls. And while I was leading my youth group in college, I was not the model Christian on the weekends. I struggled with my priorities and with balancing the lures of the world and being centered in Christ.

When I was thirty, I was married, finishing my medical residency, and starting as a professor at Duke University. I was worried about my career—what kind of papers to present and publish, and how to be accepted in academic and professional circles. And I was worried about my marriage. Ours wasn't perfect. Both of us tried to see what we could get, rather than what Christ could give.

By age forty, I was worrying about my medical practice—caring for patients, finding my way through the professional politics, and my lack of acceptance, even though I had greatly succeeded. What were my kids going to do? What about my wife? Was our marriage going to last?

At fifty, I was more concerned about holding on. The demands of work were so great that I didn't have much time for anything but to go home, rest, and work out so I could stay fit to work, read the Scripture, and pray. Life became a whole lot of just focusing on work and trying to have joy in work.

On my sixtieth birthday I looked back and was amazed at how much I had struggled with worry through the years. But I also think I learned a lot about dealing with worry. I've learned it isn't important whether I work harder or work less. It's more important for me to have enough faith in God's eternal grace so His peace and joy and contentment can blossom forth. And I've learned to be thankful that I'm alive, that I enjoy my work, that my children have done well, and that I have beautiful grandchildren. I'm thankful life has worked out as well as it has.

When I'm seventy and, God willing, eighty, I think it will continue to be the same as it's been since I was ten. I'll still be tempted to worry about being accepted by others and being successful. I'll worry about my marriage and about my children and grandchildren. I'll still struggle with worry and, at the same time, practice being continually thankful.

Complete faith and trust hasn't happened for me overnight. I wasn't permanently rid of worry when one day I said, "Lord, I'll let You do everything." Life has followed cycles of more trust and less trust, more thanksgiving and less thanksgiving, more surrender and less surrender. It's been a process of making many, many mistakes and spending a lot of time on my knees listening to and talking with God. And I still have room to grow.

When each of us crosses the line and commits our life to the Person of Jesus Christ, we're plunged into a process of transformation. We don't always make clear progress. Sometimes it's two steps forward and three back. Now we hope that the three steps back are small and that there are more steps forward overall. But we must go through all the steps as we grow in our intimacy with Christ.

We should never waver in our commitment to His process of transformation. Few things are accomplished immediately. No one can decide one day he will run a marathon the next. He must train diligently for months.

It's the same way with our spiritual transformation. We cannot be transformed in a day. But we commit to the process every day.

Life is much like the eighth round of a ten-round fight. We have to keep getting up and getting back in the ring. We might have taken hits in the past; we might have even been knocked down by events. But we need to get up every morning determined to keep going. And we need to let that persistence extend throughout the day, every day. We have to keep our focus on God, despite all the attacks we face from the world.

All of us have times in our lives when we feel up and times when we feel down. But we can't let our inner peace be destroyed by outside circumstances and events. In those down times, we still need to be filled with thanksgiving.

> I will extol the LORD at all times; his praise will always be
> on my lips.
>
> —PSALM 34:1

Our praise and thanksgiving will keep us strong in the up and down cycles we face as we are transformed by the grace of God into His character. We're all going through this process of transformation—of focusing on God and not on ourselves. The struggle against selfishness and worry is a continual one, and one that should be continued. When we accept God's call to be His children, we commit ourselves to building an intimate, personal relationship with the Person of Jesus Christ.

Growing in relationship with God is based on receiving new revelation of who He is and discovering His purpose for life. Throughout history, God has been revealing Himself to greater depths for all who will focus on Him. Old Testament saints had revelation of God through their interaction with Him. Enoch, Noah, Abraham, Moses, and others of whom we have read each experienced God in different ways. Their lives teach us who God is and how He desires to interact with His creation—mankind. Then when Christ came, He taught that His mission was to reveal the Father to us (see John 14:1–10) and to give His life as a ransom for our sin. The Book of Hebrews tells us:

> In the past God spoke to our forefathers through the prophets at many times and in various ways, but in these last days he has spoken to us by his Son, whom he appointed heir of all things, and through whom he made the universe.
>
> —HEBREWS 1:1–2

Christ became the most perfect revelation of God in the earth. It is interesting that this passage refers to the fact that it was through Christ that God made the universe. In a real sense, the phenomenal discoveries that science is making regarding the marvels of the universe are revealing the power and love of God to our generation in ways that have never been known before.

Dr. Swenson astutely observes that people who lived at the time of Christ enjoyed a special privilege: they looked God in the eye. While we do not have that physical proximity to Jesus, we have one advantage earlier people lacked: the new discoveries of science. While, Swenson admits, science hardly compares to the physical presence of Jesus or the revealed truth of the Scripture, we would be wise not to underestimate it. It provides us an advantage in spiritual perspective previous generations could hardly imagine. People of faith often tend to fear science or even dread it. "My feeling, however, is quite different. Science is thrilling. True science is a friend of Truth… Truthful science always tells us much about the power, precision, design, and sovereignty of God—details we learn nowhere else." [1] We can grow in our awe and adoration of God as we consider the wonder of the universe that He made.

Swenson concludes: "God has allowed us the privilege of living in a time when great mysteries are being uncovered. No previous era knew about quantum mechanics, relativity, subatomic particles, supernovas, ageless photons, or DNA. They all reveal the stunning genius of a God who spoke a time-space-matter-light universe into existence, balanced it with impossible requirements of precision, and then gifted it with life…Science is a close friend of the theology of sovereignty. None of these findings were understood in detail until science uncovered them. When science digs, faith rightly grows."[2]

In every way that our relationship with God grows—through studying His Word, through prayer, worship, and learning to appreciate His greatness in all of creation—we are being transformed into the image of Christ as children of God living in His kingdom:

> Now the Lord is the Spirit, and where the Spirit of the Lord is, there is freedom. And we, who with unveiled faces all reflect the Lord's glory, are being transformed into his likeness with ever-increasing glory, which comes from the Lord, who is the Spirit.
> —2 CORINTHIANS 3:17–18

This relationship is not perfected until we join God in heaven. We should never say we've attained complete transformation on earth. Our salvation doesn't make us perfect, but it does change our focus. We're still bombarded by the world and its lies and agendas. The cares and deceits of this world can easily creep in on all of us. I'm not perfect. As the license plate says, "I'm just getting better through Christ." I'm now a believer who is in the state of repentance, struggling to take my focus away from the world and place it on God. It's a constant process of focusing and refocusing. Praise God, for His grace brings us back to Him with love and kindness.

I also have this secret weapon: I know I already have ultimate victory because I believe in God and His future grace. Jesus assures us of this victory.

> I have told you these things, so that in me you may have peace. In this world you will have trouble. But take heart!

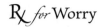

R̶ for Worry

> I have overcome the world.
>
> —JOHN 16:33

The world can throw all it wants at us; we have the ultimate partner in our corner. We have an intimate, personal relationship with the King of kings and the Lord of lords. We have victory over the world through Jesus Christ!

So why do we struggle with being thankful? Why can't we conquer worry? We're easily diverted from our focus on God because we look for satisfaction in other areas. We let our minds get cluttered with worldly attitudes and perspectives rather than the eternal perspective and values of God. Our appreciation for God falters when we lose sight of His great faithfulness and His sovereign lordship over our lives. Then our worship and adoration lag, which keeps our heart from where it longs to be—resting in His presence.

There's no question that our greatest fulfillment and peace is to be found in the unseen and the eternal. Yet it's very difficult to sustain deep faith and trust. So often we sacrifice the unseen and the eternal for the very temporary and relatively worthless activities of the present. Maintaining deep faith violates our normal, human way of thinking—of wanting to be independent and self-sufficient, desiring to take care of ourselves. Faith in God is faith in the supernatural—God's power beyond the natural world. This is not a mental trick or gimmick. We may not understand it because it's mystical. But we know, full of faith, that He helps us because He knows us. After all, He's the one who made us.

> For you created my inmost being; you knit me together in my mother's womb. I praise you because I am fearfully and wonderfully made; your works are wonderful, I know that full well. My frame was not hidden from you when I was made in the secret place. When I was woven together in the depths of the earth, your eyes saw my unformed body. All the days ordained for me were written in your

book before one of them came to be.

—PSALM 139:13–16

Remember, God created us. He didn't just create the world and set it in motion, then walk away. He was intimately involved in the creation of each of us. He has unsurpassed knowledge of us. And He is intimately involved in our transformation. Remember, the Scripture teaches that "he who began a good work in you will carry it on to completion until the day of Christ Jesus" (Phil. 1:6). He "began a good work" in us. He has started the process. He will see it through to completion.

In Hebrew 12:1, Paul compares this process with running a race. "Let us run with perseverance the race marked out for us." As a long-distance runner, I know the conditioning that's required for races. I used to run 23 miles every other day to prepare for 100-mile races. I used special instruments to condition me for higher altitudes. I ate various types of food and wore the lightest clothes for the climate. I carried special clothes in case it rained or got windy while I was training. And as race day got closer, I studied the map and plotted my course carefully.

The conditioning paid off. In one 100-mile race, I was one of only three competitors to finish. Some of the runners quit because of the snow and the cold. Others got lost. But we were prepared. Not only were we committed with our minds and our bodies, we also were committed with our hearts. We wanted to run the race and so we prepared for it.

God wants us to be prepared for the harsh conditions the world throws at us. He wants us to be ready for the times when we face the hardships, worries, or desires of the world. Because He created us, He knows how we function best.

He knows what will help us and what will hurt us. He is the Captain of our salvation and our faithful Shepherd. He is our Partner, Coach, and Guide. When we seek Him, He will reveal His plans and His vision. With our minds, hearts, and bodies we must commit to Him. The training regimen consists of the three Fs: being faithful, fervent, and focused.

Faithful

The Book of Revelation declares that one of Christ's names is "Faithful and True" (Rev. 19:11). For our lives, being faithful means being aligned to Christ; having faith not in ourselves, but in God. Faith is the essence of all our strength in God. Our faith is based in what we know. We know we have a Creator, and by the Word of God we know we have a Redeemer. We are satisfied with all that God is for us in Jesus. In faith we strive to know Him in spirit and evidence Him in our actions. We seek to take on the mind of Christ, rather than hold onto our rebellious, worldly minds.

> I want to know Christ and the power of his resurrection.
> —PHILIPPIANS 3:10

In this passage in Philippians, Paul talks about "knowing" on an intimate level. For example, in a marriage the partners "know" each other through physical, emotional, and intellectual intimacy.

In that same sort of union with Jesus Christ, everything is found in Him and our total life is committed to Him. We are with Him in our waking and our sleeping. Our lives are lived in prayer and petition; we look to Him and not to ourselves. In fact, our very first petition should be that we become intimate with Him so that by living in His presence we will constantly seek His guidance, His wisdom, His knowledge, and His strength. We know that He is real and relevant. We know His power and direction in our lives. We know He sustains us. We know Him as "Faithful and True."

Knowing Him comes through living in God's Word—the Bible. We have to be with God in the Word through the power of the Holy Spirit to grow spiritually and to carry out His work.

The Word of God is made effective in us by the Holy Spirit.

116

When the Word of God dwells in us richly, the Spirit takes that Word and makes it part of us. It transforms our minds and it shapes our desires, our focus, and our leanings.

> But his delight is in the law of the LORD, and on his law he meditates day and night. He is like a tree planted by streams of water, which yields its fruit in season and whose leaf does not wither. Whatever he does prospers.
> —PSALM 1:2–3

We need to fill ourselves with the quotations of God. Meditation on the Word every day and seeking the Lord through His Word will give us a mind-set of peace. Memorize Scripture. And then use that Scripture in your prayers. We can pray the Word back to the Lord, inserting our names. And then we can plant our feet firmly on earth and stand on those claims that are written about us as His children.

> You will keep in perfect peace him whose mind is steadfast, because he trusts in you.
> —ISAIAH 26:3

In this verse, Isaiah was implying that he had peace when he read God's Word and trusted in it, rather than trusting in his own intelligence. This was no small feat. Isaiah may have been one of the most intelligent men of the Old Testament. It may have taken a great deal of effort, will, and commitment for him to trust God first, rather than his own intellect. Isaiah's faithfulness was essential to his transformation.

If we are to have perfect peace, our minds must be fixed on God and His kingdom and not on the world. Devoting time every day to reading the Bible helps us fight worry. And one of the best ways to get the Word of God into every part of our lives is to memorize verses.

> My son, pay attention to what I say; listen closely to my words. Do not let them out of your sight, keep them

117

within your heart; for they are life to those who find them
and health to a man's whole body.

—PROVERBS 4:20–22

We are the soil and we have to be ready for the Word. May
every word be sown into us so that it gives a hundred-fold
return, and not a thousand words that give no return. Often I
have merely read many words without perceiving or receiving
their meaning and truth. Conversely, I can meditate for days
and days, for years and years, on one word. We must truly meditate on the Word and have that Word dictate the thoughts of
our hearts.

> Do not let this Book of the Law depart from your mouth;
> meditate on it day and night, so that you may be careful to
> do everything written in it. Then you will be prosperous
> and successful.
>
> —JOSHUA 1:8

Here God tells Joshua that if he follows the directions God
has written and if he is rooted in the Scripture, then God will
use Joshua to advance God's kingdom. We must be the same
way. Each day we must proclaim the Word of God, the truth
of God. We must pray it, we must say it, we must believe it,
and we must live it. That is the only way to be faithful. However, we are always conscious that our trust is in His faithfulness, not ours! He is faithful, and relying on Him stirs us up to
be faithful.

Fervent

Faith both fuels and is strengthened by our passion—fervent
desire and inner longing—for intimacy with God. We must
have the desire to be focused and aligned with Christ in a way
that truly makes us want to be healed from all the evils of the
world. That desire includes healing from worry and living in

a thanksgiving frenzy. It's a passionate cry of focusing on the Lord.

> As the deer pants for streams of water, so my soul pants for you, O God. My soul thirsts for God, for the living God.
>
> —PSALM 42:1–2

We surrender to God not out of duty, but out of love. We love Him; we embrace Him with our whole being. And we seek His presence in our lives. We seek an intimate relationship with Him. God saves us through His grace to make us like Jesus Christ, and He wants us to desire what He wants.

So the path of transformation must include fervent desire. We must desire to be transformed; we must desire to be more Christ-like. We can't just know in our heads who Christ is and how to be like Him. We must have the desire in our hearts. That fervency transforms us. We love God and are in love with Him! We're overwhelmed with thanksgiving and joy because our hearts are filled with love for the Person of Jesus Christ.

> Sing and make music in your heart to the Lord, always giving thanks to God the Father for everything, in the name of our Lord Jesus Christ.
>
> —EPHESIANS 5:19–20

If all we desire are the things of this world, we'll fall. We will fall victim to selfishness, to our independent spirits. But our passion for the living God will keep us close to Him. When love is present in a marriage, it's much easier to keep the relationship on track. When we find love in our relationship with God, growing close to Him is easier. We're lifted off this earth and freed from the cares of this world. We're engulfed in His presence and stand fast in His promises.

Focused

My cousin went through medical school. He was very bright and was successful in school. He once told me, though, that the secret to medical school was not intelligence. It was diligence. "You know, the difference between those who made it and those who didn't is sticking with it. Those who failed were quitters. They weren't dedicated enough to keep on going."

That persistence is what helps us succeed in everything. To be transformed, to become Christ-like, we must be focused on Him. We must refuse to be distracted. We must never look back, or to the left, or to the right. We must look only at Christ.

Satan would love to work on us and get us off the path. He would love for us to start feeling proud of how well we're doing in our relationships with God. He would love for us to think we have enough passion and faith to get through. He would love for us to think it's OK for us to stay where we are, that we don't need to grow any further. In fact, because we're doing so well, we might think we don't need God quite as much. Then we start slipping back into our independent, selfish natures.

We start comparing ourselves with others. We start worrying about whether we have everything we need. We take our eyes off God and start noticing the things of the world. Paul warns us to guard against this attitude and tells us how to stay focused:

> Let us throw off everything that hinders and the sin that so easily entangles, and let us run with perseverance the race marked out for us. Let us fix our eyes on Jesus, the author and perfecter of our faith, who for the joy set before him endured the cross, scorning its shame, and sat down at the right hand of the throne of God.
>
> —Hebrews 12:1–2

We have to be persistent—stubborn in our faith, stubborn in our desire, and stubborn in our determination that nothing can shake us from our focus on God. He loves us. He is faithful in His provision for us. Nothing can separate us from His love. There is no other way for us to respond than with that same determination, based in love, joy, and thanksgiving. A proper perspective of life at all times will give us that determination, helping us to appreciate the life of God that dwells in us. When compared with the temporal pleasures and possessions of this life, our eternal perspective is of ultimately more worth. It keeps us from becoming discouraged even in difficult times of life.

None of us should ever give up. We should never say we've attained perfect transformation. But through His grace we grow closer to Him through Jesus Christ. The kingdom of God will be there as we wait for Him now, as we work for Him, as we live with Jesus in our hearts, as we see what God does through us when we go forward in faith.

> Therefore, since we have been justified through faith, we have peace with God through our Lord Jesus Christ, through whom we have gained access by faith into this grace in which we now stand. And we rejoice in the hope of the glory of God.
> —ROMANS 5:1–2

When we turn our total being away from worry, when we trust in God's grace and get rid of all the worldly distractions, when we live in a thanksgiving frenzy, we are wrapped up in a cloud of exuberance transcending this world. This process of transformation keeps us focused, so that when we are ultimately translated into God's presence in heaven we'll find our exuberance multiplied immeasurably.

Discussion Questions

1. Do you worry more or worry less than you did when you were younger? Do you worry about the same things?

_____

_____

_____

2. List some ways you can practice being faithful to Christ this week.

_____

_____

_____

_____

3. How can you grow personally in your relationship with God? How do you feel passion for God's presence?

_____

_____

_____

4. What obstacles keep you from being focused on the Lord? Describe some ways you can overcome them this week.

_____

_____

_____

For further reflection

> Finally, brothers, whatever is true, whatever is noble, whatever is right, whatever is pure, whatever is lovely, whatever is admirable—if anything is excellent or praise-worthy—think about such things.
>
> —PHILIPPIANS 4:8

The process of transformation continues until we are united with God in heaven. Paul tells us how to align our thoughts to our benefit and His glory while we're earthly beings. Discuss ways you can focus on the true, noble, right, pure, lovely, and admirable qualities and blessings of the Lord.

CONCLUSION

A LECTURER WAS GIVING a talk to about four hundred students and instructors at a New England college. The lecturer asked, "How many of you look forward to a better future?" Not one person raised a hand. The audience members felt so burdened by anxiety and worry that they didn't think the future would be better. They didn't look forward with hope. Instead, they were struggling to handle the problems they faced. Their daily lives were so troubling to them, they couldn't even think about tomorrow.

Does this sound like anyone you know? I'm sure all of us, at some point in our lives, have been bogged down by problems and fears. Maybe it was a test in school, a relationship that became difficult, pressure at work, financial concerns at home, or health problems. It can feel like a bottomless pit of fear and anxiety, a pit from which we think there is no escape.

Those feelings are based on our attitude about the future. If we fear the unknown, we worry. We're afraid to make decisions, and then when we're forced to make them, we tend to make bad ones. We let events and people make us negative, critical, and unhappy. We're selfish and controlling. We're no fun to be around.

But when we have a relationship with God in the Person of Jesus Christ, we know the future. We know that we have eternity with the Author and Creator of the universe. We are engulfed by His grace today and every day. Our hearts are filled with appreciation for who He is and we trust His faithfulness to us. As we bow in worship and adoration to express our deep love and appreciation to God, He draws even closer and fills us with His eternal perspective of life. And we understand that

His sovereignty rules over all.

When we consider the greatness of God as revealed in His creation, we can rest in His infinite power and the blessed purpose He has for our lives. God does not dwell in time, but in eternity. His grace and love transcend any problem we face in time. His provision for our lives is perfect and available to all who call on His name, allowing our hearts to focus on God alone. As we grow in our appreciation of who God is, we rest more completely in His sovereignty.

Let us prize and treasure His eternity. When we look to the future knowing that God will take care of us, we're not directed by worry. We can make wise decisions because we base them on His will. We're not negative and critical. We're intercessors and caregivers. We're filled with the fruit of the Holy Spirit: love, joy, peace, patience, kindness, goodness, faithfulness, gentleness, and self-control.

As we grow in our freedom from the worries of this world, we rejoice in God always. We're filled with a spirit of thanksgiving. Thanksgiving includes *storge*, the affection and appreciation that C. S. Lewis writes about.[1] Thanksgiving includes the realization of who and what we are, and who God is. Thanksgiving is a constant state of being thankful in all things—being thankful for the glass that's half-full rather than worried about the glass that's half-empty.

Think of the many sins involved in worry: unbelief, doubt, selfishness, covetousness, and disobedience. Worry replaces God's peace with human despair. When we worry, thanksgiving is choked out by bitterness and resentment. Our noisy worry keeps us from hearing His still, small voice. We don't wait on the Lord, but we mumble about the manna He gives us. We want more and seek Him less. We doubt God's goodness, doubt His faithfulness, doubt His truthfulness, doubt His love, doubt His wisdom, and doubt His eternity.

Worry reaches beyond our own lives and starts a chain reaction in those around us. We start complaining and criticizing.

We're unpleasant, so others avoid us. We don't have joy in our own lives, which hinders the joy and peace in others.

But a spirit of thanksgiving takes the focus off ourselves and puts our lives into proper perspective with our eternal God. It gives us the proper position and purpose not only externally, but internally. We must renew this focus daily so that our spirit finds its comfort and satisfaction in the presence of God as we "enter His gates with thanksgiving and his courts with praise" (Ps. 100:4). We understand in that place of His presence that "the LORD is good and his love endures forever; his faithfulness continues through all generations" (Ps. 100:5).

Thanksgiving is the opposite of fear and worry:

> For you did not receive a spirit that makes you a slave again to fear, but you received the Spirit of sonship. And by him we cry "Abba, Father." The Spirit himself testifies with our spirit that we are God's children. Now if we are children, then we are heirs—heirs of God and co-heirs with Christ, if indeed we share in his sufferings in order that we may also share in his glory.
>
> —ROMANS 8:15–17

As believers, we are not called to live by the standards of this world and become "slaves to fear," as Paul calls it. We are called to choose a new world—a world in which we intimately know our magnificent God and experience His perfect grace. We need to be thankful forever to our God, our Creator, our heavenly Friend in this existence. His grace comes down and overshadows all our sins. As we receive salvation through Christ, the ecstasy of thanksgiving fills us when we realize He is within us and will be with us forever.

I was at a prison ministry when a speaker asked, "Are you serving time or is time serving you?" I think this applies to all of us. All we have is time. Are we filling it with anxiety, fear, and worry? Or are we filling it with thanksgiving? If we're serving time, we're just marking it; and in effect we're wasting it. We're simply enduring—wasting life by looking at it as a duty. In that mind-set, we fill a lot of time with worry because we lack hope in the future.

But if time is serving us, we're using it to strengthen our relationship with God. We're bound to God through His future grace. We are confident, courageous, and committed to Him.

We're using time to serve those around us through His power and love. We're caregivers who live out *storge* in our daily lives, supporting and appreciating others. A spirit of thanksgiving connects us to the real source of power and strength: the sovereign, faithful, eternal God.

The mental attitude we must have to use time properly is an attitude of thanksgiving unto God, a thankful spirit. Let us look at the minutes and be thankful for them. We need to treasure each moment at work and at home with our loved ones. Treasuring the present allows the peace and joy of the Lord to fill us as we anticipate the future in Him.

> Peace I leave with you; my peace I give you. I do not give to you as the world gives. Do not let your hearts be troubled and do not be afraid.
>
> —JOHN 14:27

The peace of God is different from the false peace of the world. We rest all of our hopes on the Person of Jesus Christ, who has given Himself for us. In thanksgiving, we clear our minds of the desires and agendas of the world and align ourselves with Him. He gives us eternal grace when we're engulfed with Him. He will be our appreciation, our *storge*, our desire, and our thanksgiving, now and forever.

> My mouth will speak in praise of the LORD. Let every creature praise his holy name for ever and ever.
>
> —PSALM 145:21

During long races, I quote Scriptures and go into a thanksgiving frenzy. For twenty-four to thirty hours of racing, I don't think of myself. I don't think about the race or the physical effort or let my thoughts make me tired. Instead, I focus with thanksgiving on God. I think upward. I look to Him. In the race of life, we need to think about God. We need to be full of thanksgiving for His grace and presence.

Richard Swenson describes God as the inventor of science. We can enlarge our appreciation of the greatness of God as we observe His handiwork in all of creation, which is being discovered continually by modern scientists. As we consider the wonder of our body, with its innate ability to heal itself and renew its cells continually, we should bow our hearts in adoration to our Creator-Redeemer. When we peer into the skies and consider the one hundred billion known galaxies, we are humbled by the greatness of our God and grateful for His sovereign rule over all His creation.

A thankful heart unto a sovereign God gets rid of our worry. Not just thanksgiving for our material blessings, because that may be considered self-centered; but thankfulness for God Himself which lets us be engulfed in His presence now and for eternity. Thanksgiving destroys the worried heart and leads to the peaceful heart.

God's peace is essential in the fight against worry. Sometimes we convince ourselves that we're not worried when we really are. The test is whether we have God's peace—the peace that passes all understanding (see Phil. 4:7).

This peaceful heart is the foundation for joy. We have peace with a fountain of joy springing forth when we are thankful for the sovereignty of God—His fatherly care that will provide for our entire existence through all eternity.

Thanksgiving and joy change us. Our relationships with family and friends are stronger and deeper. Our work becomes more meaningful. Thanksgiving enables us to know God. There is no better way to engage Him than by living in a thanksgiving frenzy for Him: We love Him, we worship Him, we adore Him. We enter into His presence and are engulfed by Him. We're in

His hands forever. We rest in His peace. We trust in God's eternal plan.

> "For I know the plans I have for you," declares the LORD,
> "plans to prosper you and not to harm you, plans to give
> you hope and a future."
>
> —JEREMIAH 29:11

We have eternal hope and provision in the Lord. The cares of the world can no longer weigh us down. He is God! He gives us the ultimate victory over worry!

The final answer to worry is growing in our relationship with the Lord and faith in His future grace. We must constantly thank Him and appreciate Him for His grace. Fellowship with the Person of Jesus Christ is our highest goal. Great praise and thanksgiving ensure that our relationship with Him and our love for Him are magnified every day.

What keeps us from being thankful to the Lord? Anything that clutters our minds and takes our focus off God. What keeps us from being focused on Him? Selfishness and sinfulness. We must live a life of faith in His grace. He is Lord! He is God! As believers, we are His children and He is responsible for us now and for eternity. As we look to God, His peace and presence within us make us complete. We continue to grow in our freedom from worry. We radiate with joy. Thanks be to God for His grace now and forever! Amen!

Appendix

PUTTING PROMISES INTO ACTION

ARE YOU WORRIED about a specific relationship or circumstance? This index lists some key Bible verses you can use to battle worry and fear. These verses are God's promises that He is with us and will be our support and strength. Read them. Believe them. Let His Word become the foundation in your struggles!

Are you worried, anxious, afraid, or troubled? God will give you peace.

> In my distress I called to the LORD; I cried to my God for help. From his temple he heard my voice; my cry came before him, into his ears.... He brought me out into a spacious place; he rescued me because he delighted in me.
>
> —PSALM 18:6, 19

> God is our refuge and strength, an ever-present help in trouble. Therefore we will not fear, though the earth give way and the mountains fall into the heart of the sea.
>
> —PSALM 46:1–2

> When I am afraid, I will trust in you. In God, whose word I praise, in God I trust; I will not be afraid. What can mortal man do to me?
>
> —PSALM 56:3–4

> You will keep in perfect peace him whose mind is steadfast, because he trusts in you.
>
> —ISAIAH 26:3

Do not let your hearts be troubled. Trust in God; trust also in me…Peace I leave with you; my peace I give you. I do not give to you as the world gives. Do not let your hearts be troubled and do not be afraid.

—JOHN 14:1, 27

I have told you these things, so that in me you may have peace. In this world you will have trouble. But take heart! I have overcome the world.

—JOHN 16:33

Do not be anxious about anything, but in everything, by prayer and petition, with thanksgiving, present your requests to God. And the peace of God, which transcends all understanding, will guard your hearts and your minds in Christ Jesus.

—PHILIPPIANS 4:6–7

Are you worried about the future? God will guide you.

He guides the humble in what is right and teaches them his way.

—PSALM 25:9

I will instruct you and teach you in the way you should go; I will counsel you and watch over you.

—PSALM 32:8

If the LORD delights in a man's way, he makes his steps firm; though he stumble, he will not fall, for the LORD upholds him with his hand.

—PSALM 37:23–24

Trust in the LORD with all your heart and lean not on your own understanding; in all your ways acknowledge him, and he will make your paths straight.

—PROVERBS 3:5–6

Commit to the LORD whatever you do, and your plans will succeed.

—PROVERBS 16:3

So do not fear, for I am with you; do not be dismayed, for I am your God. I will strengthen you and help you; I will uphold you with my righteous right hand.

—ISAIAH 41:10

"For I know the plans I have for you," declares the LORD, "plans to prosper you and not to harm you, plans to give you hope and a future."

—JEREMIAH 29:11

If any of you lacks wisdom, he should ask God, who gives generously to all without finding fault, and it will be given to him.

—JAMES 1:5

Are you afraid of feeling alone? God will never leave you

Be strong and courageous. Do not be afraid or terrified because of them, for the LORD your God goes with you; he will never leave you nor forsake you.

—DEUTERONOMY 31:6

Then you will call, and the LORD will answer; you will cry for help, and he will say: Here am I.

—ISAIAH 58:9

The LORD your God is with you, he is mighty to save. He will take great delight in you, he will quiet you with his love, he will rejoice over you with singing.

—ZEPHANIAH 3:17

I will not leave you as orphans; I will come to you.

—JOHN 14:18

Are you worried no one loves you?
God loves you.

For God so loved the world that he gave his one and only Son, that whoever believes in him shall not perish but have eternal life.

—JOHN 3:16

For I am convinced that neither death nor life, neither angels nor demons, neither the present nor the future, nor any powers, neither height nor depth, nor anything else in all creation, will be able to separate us from the love of God that is in Christ Jesus our Lord.

—ROMANS 8:38–39

This is how we know what love is: Jesus Christ laid down his life for us. And we ought to lay down our lives for our brothers.

—1 JOHN 3:16

This is love: not that we loved God, but that he loved us and sent his Son as an atoning sacrifice for our sins.

—1 JOHN 4:10

Are you worried that God could never forgive your sins?
God's salvation overcomes all sins and guilt.

As far as the east is from the west, so far has he removed our transgressions from us.

—PSALM 103:12

If we confess our sins, he is faithful and just and will forgive us our sins and purify us from all unrighteousness.

—1 JOHN 1:9

Do you feel depressed?
God will comfort you.

The LORD is close to the brokenhearted and saves those who are crushed in spirit.

—PSALM 34:18

Why are you downcast, O my soul? Why so disturbed within me? Put your hope in God, for I will yet praise him, my Savior and my God.

—PSALM 42:11

Are you worried because you face opposition?
God is with you.

If God is for us, who can be against us?

—ROMANS 8:31

Are you worried about physical needs?
God will provide.

Therefore I tell you, do not worry about your life, what you will eat or drink; or about your body, what you will wear. Is not life more important than food, and the body more important than clothes? Look at the birds of the air; they do not sow or reap or store away in barns, and yet your heavenly Father feeds them. Are you not much more valuable than they? Who of you by worrying can add a single hour to his life?

And why do you worry about clothes? See how the lilies of the field grow. They do not labor or spin. Yet I tell you that not even Solomon in all his splendor was dressed like one of these. If that is how God clothes the grass of the field, which is here today and tomorrow is thrown into the fire, will he not much more clothe you, O you of little faith? So do not worry, saying, "What shall we eat?" or "What shall we drink?" or "What shall we wear?" For the pagans run after all these things, and your heavenly Father knows that you need them. But seek first his kingdom and his righteousness, and all these things will be given to you as well. Therefore do not worry about tomorrow, for tomorrow will worry about itself. Each day has enough trouble of its own.

—MATTHEW 6:25–34

If you, then, though you are evil, know how to give good gifts to your children, how much more will your Father in heaven give good gifts to those who ask him!

—MATTHEW 7:11

Are not five sparrows sold for two pennies? Yet not one of them is forgotten by God. Indeed, the very hairs of your head are all numbered. Don't be afraid; you are worth more than many sparrows.

—LUKE 12:6–7

He who did not spare his own Son, but gave him up for us all—how will he not also, along with him, graciously give us all things?

—ROMANS 8:32

And God is able to make all grace abound to you, so that in all things at all times, having all that you need, you will abound in every good work.

—2 CORINTHIANS 9:8

And my God will meet all your needs according to his glorious riches in Christ Jesus.

—PHILIPPIANS 4:19

Do you worry about your safety?
God will protect you.

I will lie down and sleep in peace, for you alone, O LORD, make me dwell in safety.

—PSALM 4:8

The LORD will keep you from all harm—he will watch over your life; the LORD will watch over your coming and going both now and forevermore.

—PSALM 121:7–8

Do you worry so much that you can't sleep?
God will ease your fears.

I lie down and sleep; I wake again, because the LORD sustains me.

—PSALM 3:5

I will lie down and sleep in peace, for you alone, O LORD, make me dwell in safety.

PSALM 4:8

When you lie down, you will not be afraid; when you lie down, your sleep will be sweet.

—PROVERBS 3:24

Are you worried about your appearance?
God looks at your heart.

But the LORD said to Samuel, "Do not consider his appearance or his height, for I have rejected him. The LORD does not look at the things man looks at. Man

137

looks at the outward appearance, but the LORD looks at the heart."

—1 SAMUEL 16:7

He has made everything beautiful in its time. He has also set eternity in the hearts of men; yet they cannot fathom what God has done from beginning to end.

—ECCLESIASTES 3:11

Are you worried about your health?
God will give you strength.

A righteous man may have many troubles, but the LORD delivers him from them all.

—PSALM 34:19

The LORD will guide you always; he will satisfy your needs in a sun-scorched land and will strengthen your frame.

—ISAIAH 58:11

"But I will restore you to health and heal your wounds," declares the LORD, "because you are called an outcast, Zion for whom no one cares."

—JEREMIAH 30:17

Is any one of you sick? He should call the elders of the church to pray over him and anoint him with oil in the name of the Lord. And the prayer offered in faith will make the sick person well; the Lord will raise him up.

—JAMES 5:14–15

Are you worried about getting old?
God will stay with you.

The righteous will flourish like a palm tree, they will grow like a cedar of Lebanon; planted in the house of the LORD, they will flourish in the courts of our God. They will still bear fruit in old age, they will stay fresh and green.

—PSALM 92:12–14

Even to your old age and gray hairs I am he, I am he who will sustain you.

—ISAIAH 46:4

Are you worried about dying? God offers eternal life.

Even though I walk through the valley of the shadow of death, I will fear no evil, for you are with me; your rod and your staff, they comfort me.

—PSALM 23:4

For God so loved the world that he gave his one and only Son, that whoever believes in him shall not perish but have eternal life.

—JOHN 3:16

I give them eternal life, and they shall never perish; no one can snatch them out of my hand.

—JOHN 10:28

"Where, O death, is your victory? Where, O death, is your sting?"... Thanks be to God! He gives us the victory through our Lord Jesus Christ.

—1 CORINTHIANS 15:55, 57

Since the children have flesh and blood, he too shared in their humanity so that by his death he might destroy him who holds the power of death—that is, the devil—and free those who all their lives were held in slavery by their fear of death.

—HEBREWS 2:14–15

NOTES

INTRODUCTION

1. *Webster's Ninth New Collegiate Dictionary*, (Springfield, MA: Merriam-Webster Inc., 1990) 97.

Chapter 1

THE WORRY DISEASE

1. Charles Horace Mayo, *Aphorisms of Dr. Charles Horace Mayo, 1865–1939, and Dr. William James Mayo, 1861–1939* (Springfield, IL: Charles C. Thomas, 1951).

2. James P. Gills, *God's Prescription for Healing* (Lake Mary, FL: Siloam, 2004), 120. Further resource available by J. T. and Ruth Seamands, *Engineered for Glory* (Wilmore, KY: Francis Asbury Society, 1984).

Chapter 2

AWE, APPRECIATION, AND ADORATION

1. Ellen Vaughn, *Radical Gratitude* (Grand Rapids, MI: Zondervan, 2005) 140.

2. Ibid., 138.

Chapter 3

REALITY VS. WORRY

1. *Webster's Ninth New Collegiate Dictionary* (Springfield, Massachusetts: Merriam-Webster Inc., 1990) 980.

2. Richard Swenson, "More than Meets the Eye," DVD presentation, (Bristol, TN: Christian Medical and Dental Associations, 2005), www.cmda.org.

3. Ibid.

4. Ibid.

5. Ibid.

6. Ibid.

7. Ibid.

8. *The Westminster Shorter Catechism* can be found at http://www .shortercatechism.com.

Chapter 4

REALITY IN THE COSMOS

1. Richard Swenson, "More than Meets the Eye," DVD presentation (Bristol, TN: Christian Medical and Dental Associations, 2005), www.cmda.org.

2. Ibid.

3. Ibid.

4. Ibid.

5. Ibid.

6. Ibid.

7. Lee Strobel, *The Case for a Creator* (Grand Rapids, MI: Zondervan, 2004) 129–130.

8. Information about Allan R. Sandage can be found at http://www .petergruberfoundation.org/sandage.htm.

9. Richard Swenson, "More than Meets the Eye," DVD presentation, (Bristol, TN: Christian Medical and Dental Associations, 2005), www.cmda.org.

10. Ibid.

11. Ibid.

12. Ibid.

13. Ibid.

14. *Quantum mechanics* found at http://en.wikipedia.org/wiki/ Quantum_Mechanics.

15. Sir Arthur Eddington, biographical article found at http://www .usd.edu/phys/courses/phys300/gallery/clark/edd.html.

16. Paul Davies, "The Third Culture", found at http://www.edge
.org/3rd_culture/bios/davies.html.

17. Richard Swenson, "More than Meets the Eye," DVD presentation
(Bristol, TN: Christian Medical and Dental Associations, 2005),
www.cmda.org.

18. Ibid.

19. Ibid.

20. Ibid.

21. Ibid.

22. Ibid.

Chapter 5

A New Perspective

1. *The American Heritage Dictionary of the English Language*, third
edition (Boston: Houghton Mifflin Company, 1992).

2. Martyn Lloyd-Jones, *Be Still My Soul* (Ann Arbor, MI: Servant
Publications, 1995).

3. Martin Luther, *Three Treatises* (Philadelphia: Fortress Press, 1960).

4. Eberhard Bethge, *Dietrich Bonhoeffer* (New York: Harper and
Row, 1970).

Chapter 6

Who's in Charge?

1. B. L. Foxworthy and M. Hill, "Volcanic Eruptions of 1980 at
Mount St. Helens, The First 100 Days, U.S. Geological Survey
Professional Paper 1249," found at http://vulcan.wr.usgs.gov/
Volcanoes/MSH/Publications/PP1249/framework.html.

2. Quote available online at http://www.findquotes.com/cate_17_
History.html (accessed 10/19/06).

Chapter 7

PEACE IN GOD'S PROMISES

1. Quote available online at http://www.brainyquote.com/quotes/authors/m/mother_teresa.html (accessed 10/19/06).

2. Blaise Pascal quote available at www.thinkexist.com.

Chapter 9

THE WEAPONS AGAINST WORRY

1. Richard A. Swenson, *More Than Meets the Eye* (Colorado Springs, CO: Navpress, 2000) 115. [Robert Wearner, "Newton: Man of the Future," *Signs of the Times*, February 1999, 27; quoting I. Bernard Cohen, "Isaac Newton's Papers and Letters on Natural Philosophy," 928].

2. Ibid.

3. George Mueller, *Autobiography of George Mueller* (London: J. Nisbet and Co., 1906).

4. John Piper, *Future Grace* (Sisters, OR: Multnomah Publishers, Inc., 1995).

Chapter 10

THE BIRTH OF THE KINGDOM OF GOD

1. Archid P.McDonald, *William Barrett Travis: A Biography* (Austin, TX: Eakins Press, 1976).

Chapter 11

COURAGEOUS FAITH

1. C. S. Lewis, *The Four Loves* (NY: Harcourt Brace & Company, 1960).

2. Ibid.

3. Ibid.

Chapter 12

GROWING IN GOD

1. Richard A. Swenson, *More Than Meets the Eye*, (Colorado Springs, CO: NavPress, 2000), 184.

2. Ibid., 185.

CONCLUSION

1. C. S. Lewis, *The Four Loves* (NY: Harcourt Brace & Company, 1960).

SCRIPTURE INDEX

BIBLIOGRAPHY

Best, S. Payne. *The Venlo Incident*. London: Hutchinson, 1950.

Bethge, Eberhard. *Dietrich Bonhoeffer*. NY: Harper and Row, 1970.

Edwards, Jonathan. *The Works of Jonathan Edwards*. Edinburgh: Banner of Truth Trust, 1974, orig. 1834.

Lewis, C. S. *The Four Loves*. NY: Harcourt Brace and Company, 1960.

Lloyd-Jones, Martyn. *Be Still My Soul*. Ann Arbor, MI: Servant Publications, 1995.

Luther, Martin. *Three Treatises*. Philadelphia: Fortress Press, 1960.

Piper, John. *Future Grace*. Sisters, OR: Multnomah Publishers, Inc., 1995.

Stanley, Charles. *The Wonderful Spirit-Filled Life*. Nashville, TN: Oliver-Nelson Books, 1992.

ABOUT THE AUTHOR

J AMES P. GILLS, M.D., received his medical degree from Duke University Medical Center in 1959. He served his ophthalmology residency at Wilmer Ophthalmological Institute of Johns Hopkins University from 1962–1965. Dr. Gills founded the St. Luke's Cataract and Laser Institute in Tarpon Springs, Florida, and has performed more cataract and lens implant surgeries than any other eye surgeon in the world. Since establishing his Florida practice in 1968, he has been firmly committed to embracing new technology and perfecting the latest cataract surgery techniques. In 1974, he became the first eye surgeon in the U.S. to dedicate his practice to cataract treatment through the use of intraocular lenses. Dr. Gills has been recognized in Florida and throughout the world for his professional accomplishments and personal commitment to helping others. He has been recognized by the readers of Cataract & Refractive Surgery Today as one of the top 50 cataract and refractive opinion leaders.

As a world-renowned ophthalmologist, Dr. Gills has received innumerable medical and educational awards. In 2005, he was especially honored to receive the Duke Medical Alumni Association's Humanitarian Award. In 2007, he was blessed with a particularly treasured double honor. Dr. Gills was elected to the Johns Hopkins Society of Scholars and was also selected to receive the Distinguished Medical Alumnus Award, the highest honor bestowed by Johns Hopkins School of Medicine. Dr. Gills thereby became the first physician in the country to receive high honors twice in two weeks from the prestigious Johns Hopkins University in Baltimore.

In the years 1994 through 2004, Dr. Gills was listed in The Best

Doctors in America. As a clinical professor of ophthalmology at the University of South Florida, he was named one of the best Ophthalmologists in America in 1996 by ophthalmic academic leaders nationwide. He has served on the Board of Directors of the American College of Eye Surgeons, the Board of Visitors at Duke University Medical Center, and the Advisory Board of Wilmer Ophthalmological Institute at Johns Hopkins University. Listed in Marquis' Who's Who in America, Dr. Gills was Entrepreneur of the Year 1990 for the State of Florida, received the Tampa Bay Business Hall of Fame Award in 1993, and was given the Tampa Bay Ethics Award from the University of Tampa in 1995. In 1996, he was awarded the prestigious Innovators Award by his colleagues in the American Society of Cataract and Refractive Surgeons. In 2000, he was named Philanthropist of the Year by the National Society of Fundraising Executives, was presented with the Florida Enterprise Medal by the Merchants Association of Florida, was named Humanitarian of the Year by the Golda Meir/Kent Jewish Center in Clearwater, and was honored as Free Enterpriser of the Year by the Florida Council on Economic Education. In 2001, The Salvation Army presented Dr. Gills their prestigious "Others Award" in honor of his lifelong commitment to service and caring.

Virginia Polytechnic Institute, Dr. Gills' alma mater, presented their University Distinguished Achievement Award to him in 2003. In that same year, Dr. Gills was appointed by Governor Jeb Bush to the Board of Directors of the Florida Sports Foundation. In 2004, Dr. Gills was invited to join the prestigious Florida Council of 100, an advisory committee reporting directly to the governor on various aspects of Florida's public policy affecting the quality of life and the economic well-being of all Floridians.

While Dr. Gills has many accomplishments and varied interests, his primary focus is to restore physical vision to patients and to bring spiritual enlightenment through his life. Guided by his strong and enduring faith in Jesus Christ, he seeks to encourage and comfort the patients who come to St. Luke's and to share his faith whenever possible. It was through sharing his insights with patients that he initially began writing on Christian topics. An avid student of the Bible for many years, he now has authored nineteen books on Christian living, with over eight million copies in print. With the exception of the Bible, Dr. Gills' books are the most widely requested books in the U.S. prison system. They have been supplied to over two thousand prisons and jails, including every death row facility in the nation. In addition, Dr. Gills has published more than 195 medical articles and has authored or coauthored ten medical reference textbooks. Six of those books were bestsellers at the American Academy of Ophthalmology annual meetings.

As an ultra-distance athlete, Dr. Gills participated in forty-six marathons, including eighteen Boston marathons and fourteen 100-mile mountain runs. In addition, he completed five Ironman Triathlons in Hawaii and holds the record for completing six Double Ironman Triathlons, each within the thirty-six hour maximum time frame. Dr. Gills has served on the National Board of Directors of the Fellowship of Christian Athletes and, in 1991, was the first recipient of their Tom Landry Award. A passionate athlete, surgeon, and scientist, Dr. Gills is also a member of the Explorers Club, a prestigious, multi-disciplinary society dedicated to advancing field research, scientific exploration, and the ideal that it is vital to preserve the instinct to explore.

Married in 1962, Dr. Gills and his wife, Heather, have raised two children, Shea and Pit. Shea Gills Grundy, a former attorney and now full-time mom, is a graduate of Vanderbilt University and Emory Law School. She and her husband, Shane Grundy M.D., have four children: twins Maggie and Braddock, Jimmy, and Lily Grace. The Gills' son, J. Pit Gills, M.D., ophthalmologist, received his medical degree from Duke University Medical Center and, in 2001, joined the St. Luke's practice. "Dr. Pit" and his wife, Joy, have three children: Pitzer, Parker, and Stokes.

THE WRITINGS OF JAMES P. GILLS, M.D.

A BIBLICAL ECONOMICS MANIFESTO (WITH RON H. NASH, PH.D.)
The best understanding of economics aligns with what the Bible teaches on the subject.
ISBN: 978-0-88419-871-0
E-book ISBN: 978-1-59979-925-4

BELIEVE AND REJOICE: CHANGED BY FAITH, FILLED WITH JOY
Observe how faith in God can let us see His heart of joy.
ISBN: 978-1-59979-169-2
E-book ISBN: 978-1-61638-727-3

COME UNTO ME: GOD'S CALL TO INTIMACY
Inspired by Dr. Gills' trip to Mt. Sinai, this book explores God's eternal desire for mankind to know Him intimately.
ISBN: 978-1-59185-214-8
E-book ISBN: 978-1-61638-728-0

DARWINISM UNDER THE MICROSCOPE: HOW RECENT SCIENTIFIC EVIDENCE POINTS TO DIVINE DESIGN (WITH TOM WOODWARD, PH.D.)
Behold the wonder of it all! The facts glorify our Intelligent Creator!
ISBN: 978-0-88419-925-0
E-book ISBN: 978-1-59979-882-0

THE DYNAMICS OF WORSHIP
Designed to rekindle a passionate love for God, this book gives the *who, what, where, when, why,* and *how* of worship
ISBN: 978-1-59185-657-3
E-book ISBN: 978-1-61638-725-9

Exceeding Gratitude for the Creator's Plan: Discover the Life-Changing Dynamic of Appreciation

Standing in awe of the creation and being secure in the knowledge of our heavenly hope, the thankful believer abounds in appreciation for the Creator's wondrous plan.
ISBN: 978-1-59979-155-5
E-book ISBN: 978-1-61638-729-7

God's Prescription for Healing: Five Divine Gifts of Healing

Explore the wonders of healing by design, now and forevermore.
ISBN: 978-1-59185-286-5
E-book ISBN: 978-1-61638-730-3

Imaginations: More Than You Think

Focusing our thoughts will help us grow closer to God.
ISBN: 978-1-59185-609-2
E-book ISBN: 978-1-59979-883-7

Love: Fulfilling the Ultimate Quest

Enjoy a quick refresher course on the meaning and method of God's great gift.
ISBN: 978-1-59979-235-4
E-book ISBN: 978-1-61638-731-7

Overcoming Spiritual Blindness

Jesus + anything = nothing. Jesus + nothing = everything. Here is a book that will help you recognize the many facets of spiritual blindness as you seek to fulfill the Lord's plan for your life.
ISBN: 978-1-59185-607-8
E-book ISBN: 978-1-59979-884-4

Resting in His Redemption

We were created for communion with God. Discover how to rest in His redemption and enjoy a life of divine peace.
ISBN: 978-1-61638-349-7
E-book ISBN: 978-1-61638-425-8

Rx for Worry: A Thankful Heart

Trust your future to the God who is in eternal control.
ISBN: 978-1-59979-090-9
E-book ISBN: 978-1-59979-926-1

The Prayerful Spirit: Passion for God, Compassion for People

Dr. Gills tells how prayer has changed his life as well as the lives of patients and other doctors. It will change your life also!

ISBN: 978-1-59185-215-5
E-book ISBN: 978-1-61638-732-7

The Unseen Essential: A Story for Our Troubled Times...
Part One

This compelling, contemporary novel portrays one man's transformation through the power of God's love.

ISBN: 978-1-59185-810-2
E-book ISBN: 978-1-59979-513-3

Tender Journey: A Story for Our Troubled Times...
Part Two

Be enriched by the popular sequel to *The Unseen Essential*.

ISBN: 978-1-59185-809-6
E-book ISBN: 978-1-59979-509-6

DID YOU ENJOY THIS BOOK?

We at Love Press would be pleased to hear from you if

Rx for Worry

has had an effect on your life or the lives of your loved ones.

Send your letters to:

Love Press
P.O. Box 1608
Tarpon Springs, FL 34688-1608